ANTIQUES FOR·ALL

Adrian Vincent

Ravette London

Text design by Christine Lloyd

First published by Ravette Limited, 1986
©1986, Ravette Limited

ISBN 0 948456 04 3

Printed and bound for Ravette Limited,
3 Glenside Estate, Star Road, Partridge
Green, Horsham, Sussex RH13 8RA by
Mateu Cromo Artes Gráficas, s.a.

LIST OF CONTENTS

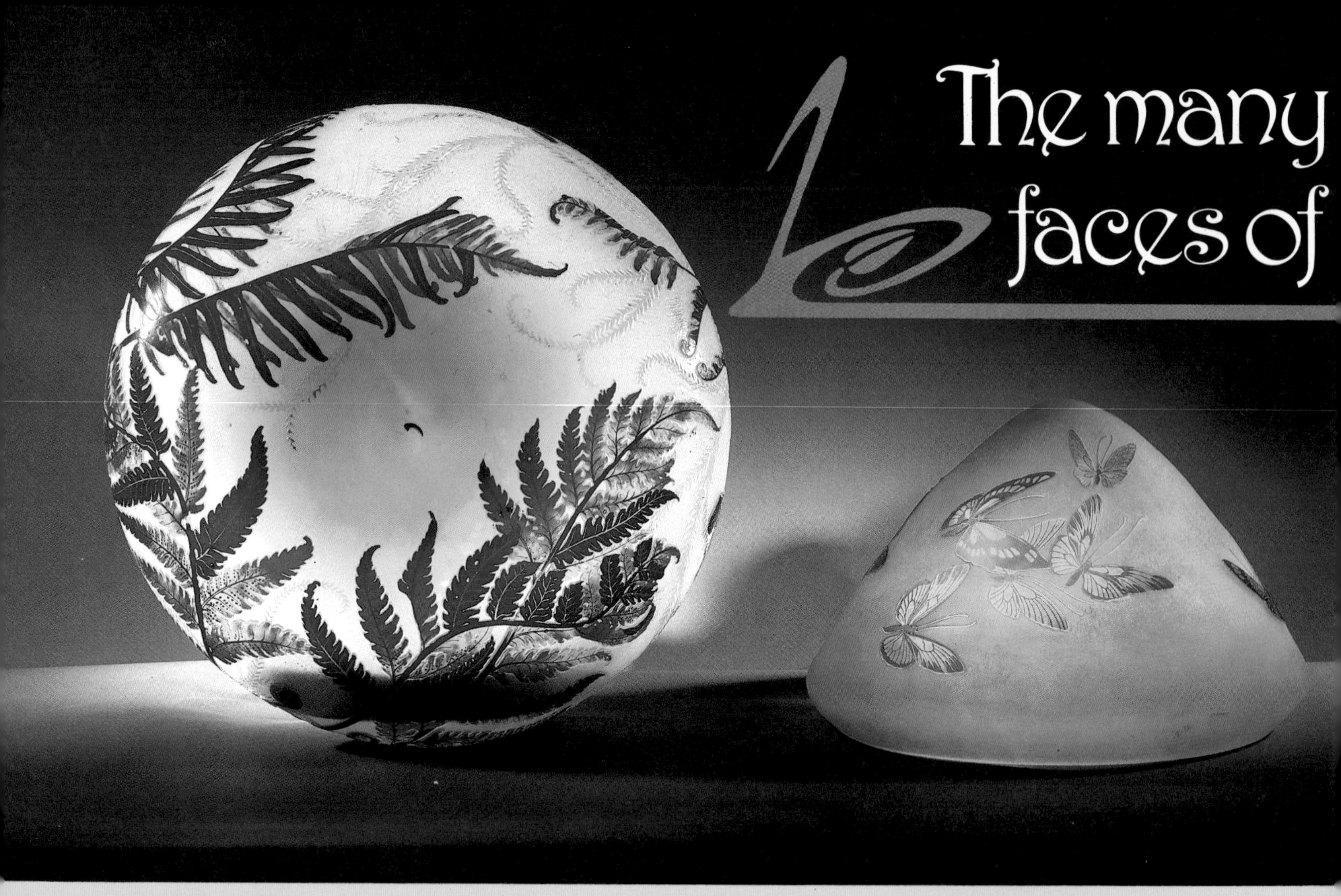

Above: *Two large cameo shades by Gallé, leading French glassmaker and outstanding exponent of Art Nouveau.*
Right: *Two outstanding glass table lamps by Auguste Daum, a glassmaker, whose factory at Nancy, produced vases and lamps in the manner of Gallé.*

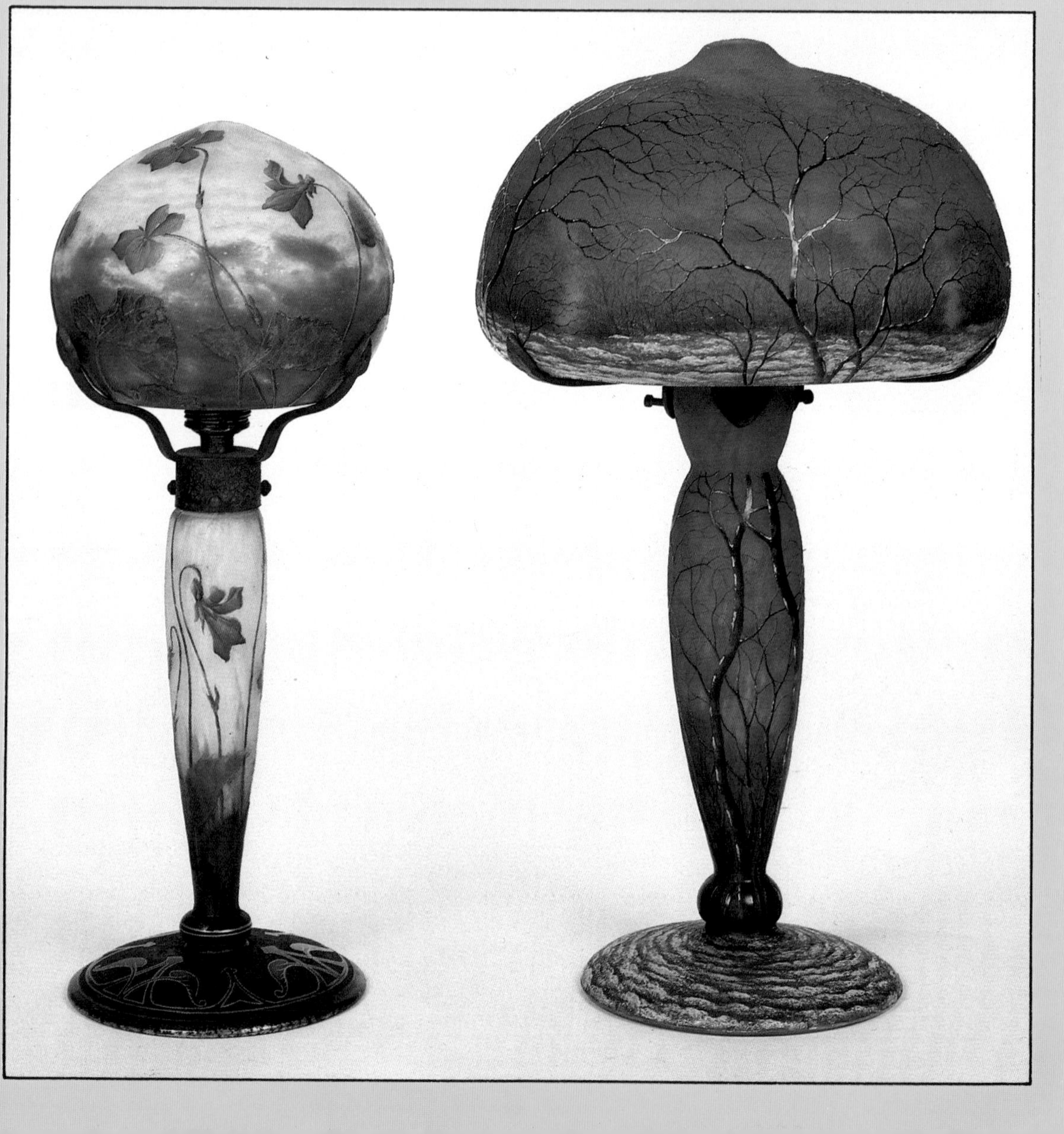

Art Nouveau

Walter Crane, the English painter and illustrator, described art nouveau as a 'strange decorative disease'. To that prudish section of Victorian society that deplored the excesses of this new exotic art form which was over fond of using outlines which suggested the form of a naked woman, it must certainly have seemed like a disease, and a contagious one at that, which had spread across Europe and then over to America with incredible rapidity.

Art Nouveau as an art form had begun to appear in the 1880s, though it was not called that until 1895, when it was named after an art gallery called the Maison de l'Art Nouveau, which had been opened in the same year by Samuel Bing, a wealthy art dealer of German extraction, who had already made something of a reputation for himself by displaying the more *avant garde* works of contemporary artists.

The movement, however, was started in Britain by Arthur Mackmurdo, when he had brought out a book in 1883 called *Wren's City Churches*, which had a revolutionary front page design and is the earliest example of art nouveau we have.

Influenced to some degree by Japanese art, the new movement took its shapes from nature and marine life, interweaving flowers and insects in its designs for pottery, jewellery, glass and even furniture. Its practitioners were also highly innovative in the way they used their materials. Potters began to produce china that resembled the swirling forms of drapery, the furniture makers, often using local fruitwoods, used thistles and cow parsley as decorative motifs, would carve legs in the shape of plants, while the jewellers went in for designing the most intricate and often bizarre looking pieces. All this, as can be imagined, met with disapproval in many circles, where the ideal art form was something solid and respectable looking. As for the glass of Émile Gallé, with his illuminated glass flowers sprouting out of electric lamps, or his vases with a few lines of Baudelaire — well, these could be described only as frivolous or decadent. Fortunately for posterity, this view was not shared by the majority of people.

Émile Gallé was not only the most well known, but also the finest of all the glass makers of the period. Gallé's virtuosity with glass included cameo carving and colour fusion, enamelling and making opaque glass, to name just a few of the techniques he used in the making of glass. Some of his work involved the use of so many techniques at one time that it is difficult to see where one effect begins and another ends.

All Gallé's personal work is signed; those made by his factory in Nancy are marked

Right above: *A Gallé enamelled glass Jardiniere with bronze base.*
Below: *One of a pair of Gallé cameo glass plafonniers.*

'cristallerie d'Émile Gallé'. After his death at a relatively early age of 54 in 1904, the factory continued production until the outbreak of World War I. It started up again after the war and continued production until 1935.

It is important to note that Gallé glass which has a star beside the name Gallé were produced after his death, and are vastly inferior to those made earlier.

It should be added that Gallé did not confine his creative activities to glass. Venturing into the field of furniture making in which he often used marquetry, he tried, not too successfully, to combine his creative flair with the not unnatural desire to produce a commercial commodity. Sometimes there is a certain

Left: A French walnut art nouveau display cabinet.
Below from left to right:
A) An art nouveau pendant, probably Austrian, fashioned as a teardrop-shaped plaque of bone ivory applied with silver coloured leaves and flowers set with small coral cabochons.
B) German foliate pendant embellished with scrolls and leaves set with oval plaques of mother-o' pearl and a central faceted citrine.
C) An enamelled pendant with a pierced and chased group of three leaved clover against a red enamelled plaque within a foliate band set with foil backed garnets and having three garnet set drops.
D) A pendant cast with a central winged figure holding the Holy Grail, flanked by amethyst cabochons in beaded collets.

heaviness to his designs which are redeemed by his wonderful use of marquetry.

Better and more famous cabinet makers of the art nouveau period were Louis Mojorelle, who applied all the old traditions of cabinet making to the new art form with far more success than Gallé. The other cabinet maker was Hector Guimard, whose furniture had a purity of line to it not often matched by other cabinet makers of the period. It was Guimard who designed the Paris Metro entrances in 1900, which were disliked by the public at the time.

Gallé had many imitators, but very few of them came anywhere near to matching the quality of his glass work. Nevertheless, a number of glass makers were around in France who were producing some excellent pieces of glass, particularly the brothers Auguste and Antonin Daum, who also had a factory at Nancy. Although their designs were less extravagant than those of Gallé, their vases decorated with landscape scenes were of a rare quality, and are much sought after by collectors today.

Meanwhile, in the suburbs of Paris, the Cristallerie de Pantin, under the direction of J.F. Legras, was also producing vases decorated with landscape or woodland scenes, as well as etched and deeply cut glass that often bore the name De Vez, the pseudonym of Camille de Verreux, the art director of the company. Occasionally other art nouveau glass makers' pieces turn up in the auction rooms, such as the work of Albert Dammouse and Francois Decorchemont, who died in 1971, after living to the ripe old age of 91. Decorchemont specialised in making decorative objects in pate de verre (powdered glass mixed with an adhesive to make a glass paste). Dammouse, who had begun his career working as a potter at the Sevres factory, used this technique with added floral decorations.

In the same way that Gallé had become the

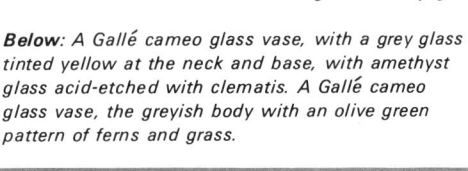

Far left: A Mucha poster.

Left: A Zsiknay lustre vase.

Below left: French silver mounted glass claret jug.

Below: A Gallé cameo glass vase, with a grey glass tinted yellow at the neck and base, with amethyst glass acid-etched with clematis. A Gallé cameo glass vase, the greyish body with an olive green pattern of ferns and grass.

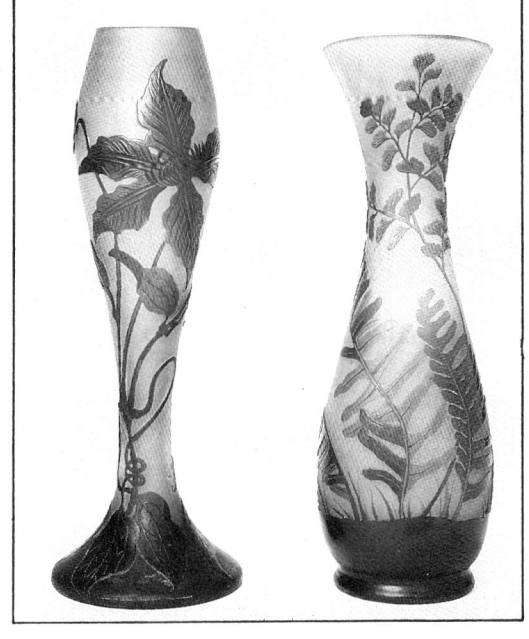

leading exponent in making art nouveau glass, René Lalique was to become the leading designer of art nouveau jewellery. On a small scale, his work was probably the finest expression of the form. Although it has not the same obvious display value as the larger pieces of art nouveau in other fields, his work was greatly appreciated by many notable figures of the time, including Sarah Bernhardt, who wore a number of his creations around her neck. Calouste Gulbenkien, the Armenian millionaire, who had met Lalique through Bernhardt, made an invaluable contribution to the arts when he commissioned a collection of 145 pieces of jewellery from Lalique. This magnificent collection can now be seen at the Paombel Palace, near Lisbon, and is matched only by the collection of art nouveau jewellery housed in the Musee des Arts Decoratifs in Paris, which is regrettably hidden away in the vaults for security reasons. Although Lalique had some thirty craftsmen working for him at one time, pieces by him are hard to come by. Why this should be is something of a mystery.

Art Nouveau silver was also produced in France, but to see it at its best we have to return to England, where the Arts and Crafts movement, devoted to the promotion of hand craftsmanship had given impetus to the craft of the silversmith.

Two refugees from the movement, which had immediately preceded Art Nouveau, were C.R. Ashbee, and Christopher Dresser who had started off as a botanist before turning to the decorative arts, made a number of interesting designs in silver and E.P.N.S. which were somewhat ahead of their time with their emphasis on uncluttered lines and geometrical forms. Mention must be made also of Charles Voysey, who had designed everything from large pieces of furniture to jewellery. His silver owes much to the Arts and Craft Movement, of which he was a founder member.

The London store of Libertys, who had always been a supporter of any new art form that showed commercial possibilities, added to the popularity of the art nouveau silver by bringing out their 'Cymric' line, which had been influenced by some of Ashbee's designs based on Celtic jewellery in which the blue of turquoise enamels or stones was often used for ornamentation.

In the field of cabinet making, the most *avant garde* work was done in Belgium where a number of young cabinet makers known as Les Vingt (The Twenty) had begun making a revolutionary form of art nouveau furniture, often made from woods imported from the Congo. The three leading members of the group were Henri van de Velde, Victor Horta and Gustave Serrurier-Bovay. The group aimed to produce architectural furniture that harmonised with the interior of a house, which meant, of course, that any individual piece of furniture could not stand on its own merit. Often their ideas were carried to such an extreme that they seem almost laughable today. Serrurier-Bovay designed a suite of completely collapsible

furniture held together with clamps — useful for when moving house — but for precious little else — while Van de Velde's contribution to the scene was to decorate a tobacco shop known as the Magazin Habana, which looked more like something from the German expressionistic film, *The Cabinet of Dr. Caligari,* than the harmonious and restful creation it was meant to be.

Horta's masterpiece was undoubtedly the Maison Tassel in Brussels, in which all the most characteristic elements of art nouveau were fused into an harmonious whole, with a tangle of whiplash curves forming a single *leitmotif.* His belief that ornament was an essential part of the architecture of a house was carried to its ultimate here in a dazzling display of virtuosity which, frankly, becomes a little too overpowering for modern taste.

When art nouveau reached America, it expressed itself in two highly popular forms — in graphics and in the glass of Louis Comfort Tiffany, who was the owner of the most fashionable jeweller's shop in America. Before the arrival of art nouveau in the country, Tiffany had already acquired a large collection of glass which was to spur him on to learn as much as he could about the subject. After a great deal of study, Tiffany was able to patent a form of glass known as favrile, which involved introducing an iridescent appearance to glass. By using various forms of oxide, he was able also to create a number of startling colours which were to become a distinctive feature of much

of Tiffany's work. Not content with that he went on to make an equally distinctive gold lustre, in which he used twenty five gold dollar pieces as its base, Tiffany was never one to stint on the cost in his search for perfection.

The consequence of all this when it actually came to the making of his glass, was to make a Tiffany piece immediately recognisable. But for all that, it was his leaded lamp shades that were to make him an internationally famous figure.

The Tiffany lamp stands were made in a number of forms, ranging from those whose shades imitated stained glass, to even more elaborate pieces that might resemble a wisteria

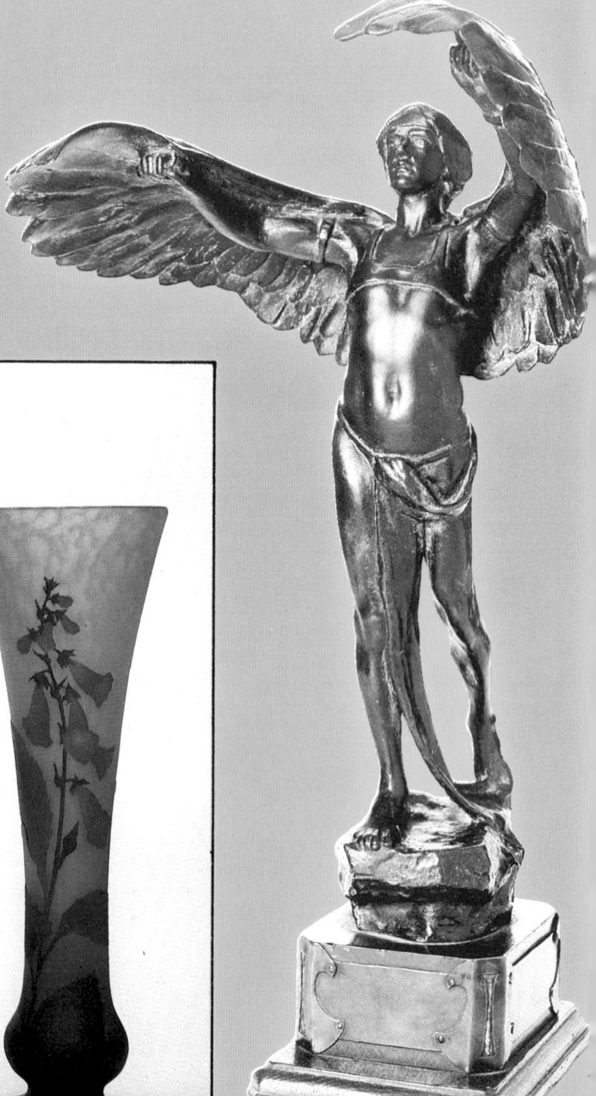

Above. Three Daum 'landscape' vases. Another painted with red currants and leaves.
Below. From left to right: A large Daum Cameo Glass vase. A Legras Oviform Vase. Two Daum glass vases.
Right: A bronze figure 'Icarus'. Probably the work of Alexander Fisher, a sculptor and enamelist. *Phillips.*

tree, or be decorated with dragon flies. In their time, Tiffany lamps were very much in vogue, and still are, if one may judge by the copies of them that can be seen in almost every electrical shop today. Tiffany remains one of the most significant figures in the development of art nouveau. It has to be added that not all the Tiffany lamps that bear his name were actually made by him. Also, a large number of them were turned out on a commercial basis, which meant that the standard of workmanship varied slightly from time to time.

In the decorative arts, the American art nouveau poster and book jacket designs were influenced by a number of other artists ranging from Toulouse-Lautrec to Walter Crane and Aubrey Beardsley, and with more than a passing nod also given to Eugene Grasset, who is best known for his French theatre posters, and whose work was an expression of art nouveau in its purest form. Some of the American artists, however, still managed to find a style that was essentially American, while continuing to pay homage to the art nouveau movement.

By 1910, the art nouveau movement was dead and almost completely forgotten, which seems strange when one remembers that there was hardly a single art form which had not come under its influence. One can only be grateful that so much of it still exists for us to enjoy.

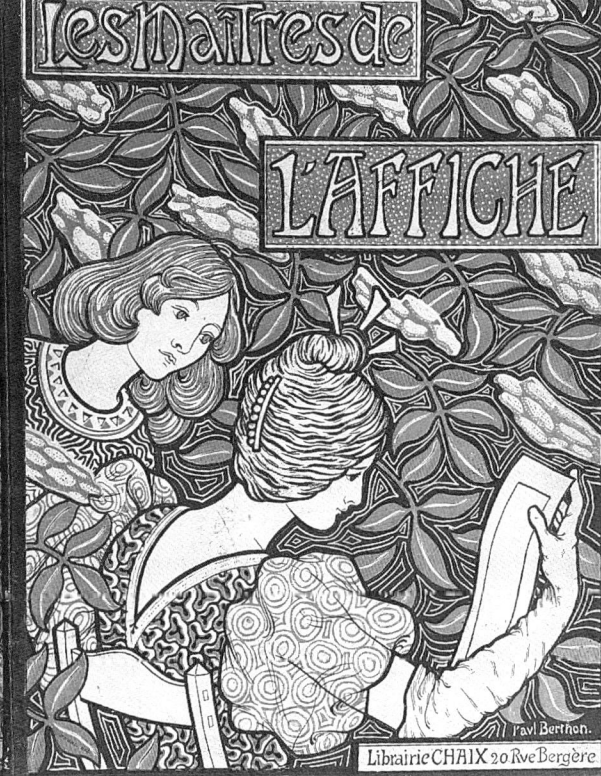

Left: An art nouveau print from a set of five volumes, 'Les Maitres de L'Affiche, by Paul Berthon, published between 1896 and 1900.
Below left: 'The Bather' A Royal Doulton stoneware figure, designed by John Broad.

Below: A bronze and ivory garniture, the tusks in the form of flutes.

SILHOUETTES

When Etienne de Silhouette, the controller of Finance in the France of Louis XV died in 1769, his passing was not greatly regretted, as he had been much disliked for his meaness. The fact that he achieved a minor sort of immortality was an accident. Because his name was used as a definition of meaness, the term silhouette began to be used for the scissor cutting art of profiles, which had become the craze of Europe and America. It was, after all, a much cheaper way of having one's portrait executed, than having a painting done in oils or watercolour.

Actually, the origins of the silhouette goes back a long way, but it did not become a popular art form until the 18th century, when it flourished greatly between the years of 1760 and 1860. Many famous people, including Royalty became adept scissor cutters.

Apart from free-hand scissor-cutting, various other methods were used to creat silhouettes. A candle would be used to cast a shadow on a large screen, the outline drawn, and then a device known as a 'pantograph' used to reduce the size before it was cut. Other methods involved the use of black ink on white board, or covering flat glass with black paint, outlining the profile with a sharp point, and thereafter, scraping away the surround. Silhouettes were also used to decorate porcelain, and appeared on commemorative pieces from widely varying factories, ranging from Bristol and Worcester, to Dresden and Nymphenburg.

The silhouette was rescued from going into a decline largely by the efforts of Augustin Edouart, who published his *Treatise* on the subject in 1835. Edouart was a French refugee who came to England in 1814 and became one of the greatest of all the silhouette cutters, cutting an enormous number of likenesses before he died in 1861. But surpassing him was John Miers, who died in 1821. Although another prolific artist, his silhouettes were extremely delicate.

The Americans also produced silhouettes by the thousand, and their work has often served as a valuable source of reference, as their silhouettes are the only pictures we have of a number of American historical figures of that period.

The Continent also produced a large number of scissor artists, particularly in Germany, Austria and France.

At the other end of the artistic scale were the poor man's miniatures, in which the sitter's portrait was done in a minute or two, for a few shillings.

Silhouettes generally showed only the head, always in profile, though Edouart and a few others, later produced full length figures. Group figures like the one shown below were rare.

Silhouettes which were incidentally called 'shades' before Edouart introduced the word into England, were eventually produced by machines. The final death knell was given to the silhouette by the photograph.

Prices for silhouettes today vary enormously. Edouart's silhouettes are generally at the top end of the market.

Top left. Young boy. Circa 1835.
Below. The Sharpin family of Scarborough by Augustin Edouart. Bottom. Three silhouettes by J. Holmes.
Opposite page. Sporting and comic silhouettes. Centre. Silhouettes painted in indian ink and touched with gold. The rest are various notables of their time.

The technique for making millefiori had been known
for many centuries. But it was left to a number of
19th century French craftsmen to bring it to its
ultimate expression.

Although the making of paper weights by the *millefiori* technique goes back to the days of Imperial Rome, the French have the honour of developing their making of them to a fine art, which has never been equalled by any other country. The factories concerned in their making were Baccarat, Clichy and St. Louis, who began producing them from the middle of the 19th century, thanks mainly to a Venetian glass manufacturer named Pietro Bigaglia, who had displayed a number of his own paperweights at the Exhibition of Austrian Industry in Vienna in 1845.

St. Louis, a factory with a glass making history of over 400 years, was the first to see the selling potential, and began making their own weights, which are now eagerly sought after by collectors.

The earliest recorded weight from the St. Louis factory is dated 1845, and the latest 1849. Their production was stopped, actually in 1850, but the factory started producing again in 1967.

The Baccarat weights date from between 1846 and 1849, and often incorporate the

date of manufacture in their design. Reptiles, fruit, vegetables, flowers and butterflies, were all popular subjects and are noted for the clearness of their glass and their rich colours. More rarely, they incorporated a cameo in the weight. In 1952, they resumed production, and are now producing some 300 weights a year.

The Clichy factory produced weights until 1885, when they ceased production. Unfortunately, few records of the Clichy factory were kept, so not a great deal is known about their history. A design known as the 'Clichy Rose', was a hallmark of their work, which also included a quite unique series with caterpillars.

The first English paperweights were actually produced before the French factories went into production.

*Above. An important and very
rare baccarat snake paperweight.*

In 1819 Apsley Pellatt, the son of a London glass warehouse owner took out a patent for making glass incrustations. Two years later, he started his own glasshouse in Falcon Street, Southwark, where he began producing weights, which involved coating medallions and cameos with a thick layer of clear glass. A well-known figure in his time, he lectured on the history of glass making and wrote two books on the subject: 'Glass Manufacturers', and 'Curiosities of Glass Making'. An example of his work can be seen in the Victoria and Albert Museum.

However, English paperweights in the French manner did not appear until 1845, when a factory in Stourbridge in Wilts., began producing them. The early ones were somewhat crude, and it was not until 1848, that they were able to produce anything that could begin to compare with the French paperweights. By then, other factories in England had also began producing weights, notably George Bacchus and Sons in Birmingham, who made something of a name for themselves after their coloured table ware had been seen at the Great Exhibition of 1851. But the English weights never really matched the quality of the French weights.

A number of American glass making factories were also involved in the making of paperweights during the 19th century — perhaps with more success than their English counterparts. As well as copying the French designs, most of them also created their own designs. The two major companies producing weights were the New England Glass Company and the Boston and Sandwich Glass Company in Massachusetts.

The process of making a *millefiori* weight demands a great deal of patience and skill. The canes of glass which are going to be used to make the patterns, are first heated and then dipped a number of times into molten glass of varying colours. The canes are then stretched and thinned until the sections are of the required length. After they have been cut, they are arranged in the desired pattern on a piece of thin glass. Softened mould is placed over the whole and molten glass is then poured in. Afterwards it is dipped in molten glass and shaped. Great care is particularly needed to maintain the temperatures throughout the process, otherwise cracks will result.

All the 19th century paperweights are much sought after, especially the French weights decorated with a single subject. The weights from the French factories now fetch staggering prices running into thousands of pounds. And yet not so long ago, in 1970 to be exact, a Clichy and St. Louis were sold in auction for £190 and £130 respectively. Baccarats could still be bought then for sums under £200. Like most other things in the field of antiques, prices have soared.

If you are in a position to buy these beautiful objects, and wish to start collecting them, make sure you know something about them first, and then go to a reputable dealer. (This applies to almost everything when buying expensive antiques).

To tell the difference between an antique and modern weight is quite difficult and really needs a trained eye, which can only be obtained by studying them at length in museum collections.

Although British weights, such as the Scottish Caithness weights are among some of the best examples of modern weights produced in this country, a large number of weights have been produced which are poorly made, but not so badly made as not to fool someone who knows nothing about them.

Even when you have the genuine article in your hands, they should be examined for scratches. Although these can be removed, it is best to leave the weight alone, even if it is offered at what seems a bargain price.

WHERE TO BUY

Ranklin, Best and Green Ltd., The London Glass Centre, 293-5 Kingsland Road, London E8.
Spink and Son Ltd., 5-7 King Street, London SW1.
Maureen Thompson, 34 Kensington Church Street, London W8.
Note: All the major auction rooms have the occasional sale of paper weights.

MUSEUMS

Bristol City Art Gallery.
Farnham Museum, Farnham.
Hungerford: Littlecote House.
Swansea: Glynn Vivian Art Gallery.

BOOKS

England:
Glass Paperweights Patricia McCawley.
Glass Paperweights from France by Patricia McCawley.
U.S.A.
Glass Paperweights of the Bergstrom Art Centre by Patricia K. McCawley.
One Hundred of the Most Important Paperweights by Paul Jokelson.

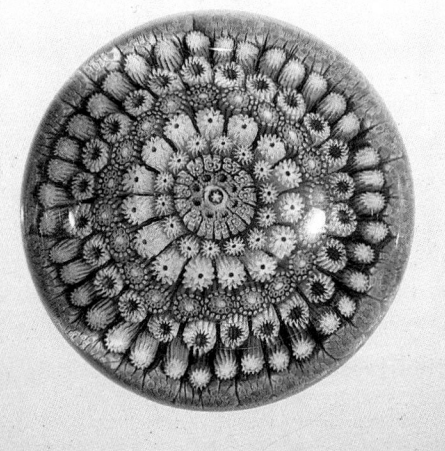

A collection of French mid-19th century paperweights.

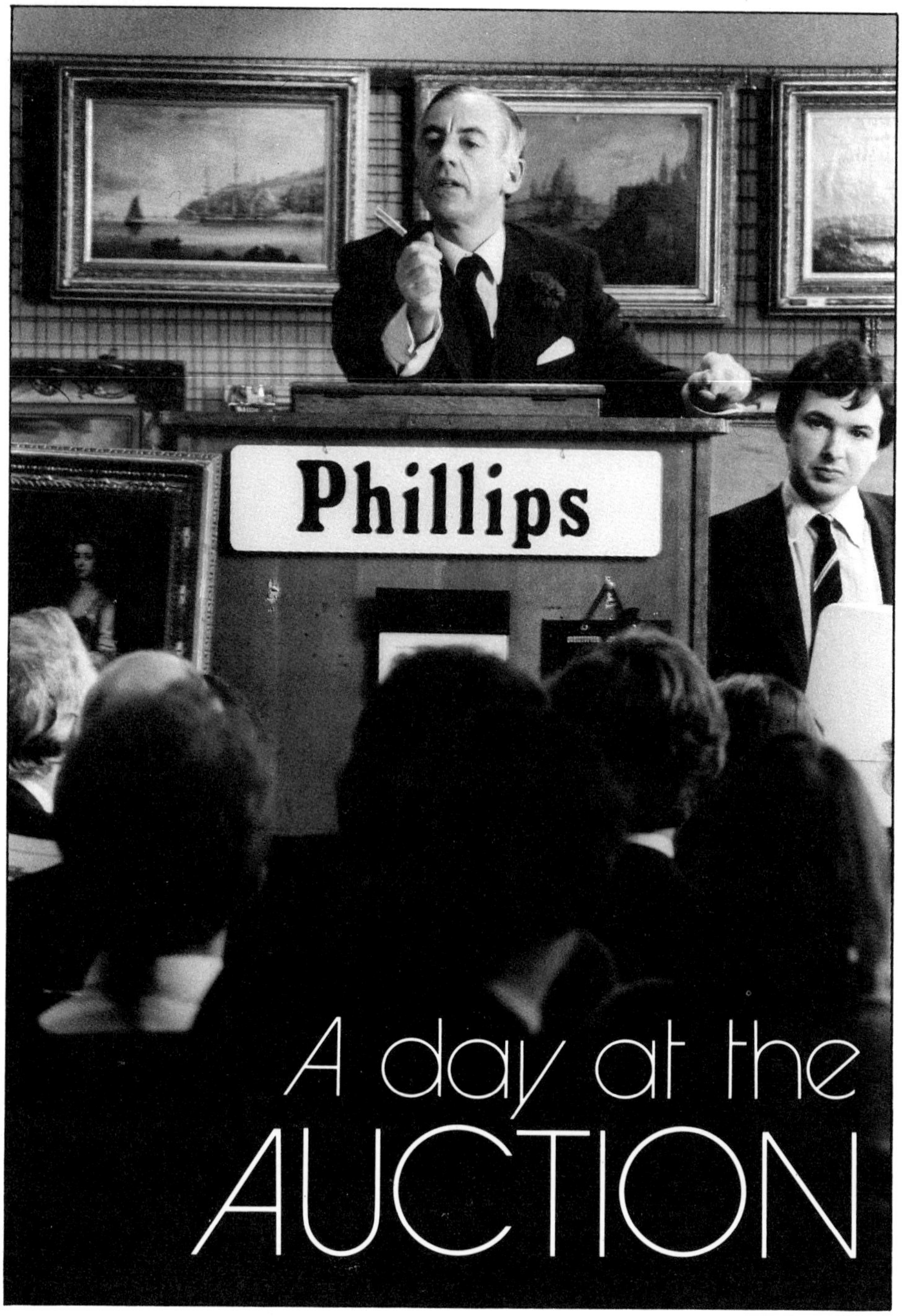

A day at the AUCTION

Contrary to some people's ideas about attending auction rooms, you will not find that you have suddenly acquired some highly expensive object by scratching your nose.

There must be thousands of people who have peeked in an auction room while a sale is on, and then promptly fled. No doubt the authoritarian air of the auctioneer, the assured way the people seem to be bidding and the actual speed of the bidding, must be rather frightening to anyone attending an auction sale for the first time. But there is really nothing to worry about. Whatever happens, the newcomer to an auction room will not suddenly find they have just bought some highly expensive antique by having made some careless gesture which has been misinterpreted by the auctioneer as a bid.

Actually, the bidding procedure at most auctions is a very simple one. But if you decide to visit an auction with the serious intention of buying, you should first attend one of the viewings, which are generally held a couple of days before the auction. This will give you a chance to examine at leisure the articles that will be on sale. The catalogue, which you can buy at the door or front desk, will describe the article, date it where possible, and give you an estimate of what it is likely to fetch. The latter, it should be added, is not an infallible guide, as items often fetch more (or less) than estimated.

When you have decided on the items you are going to bid for, decide also exactly how much you are prepared to bid, allowing at the same time just one extra bid above that figure: there is nothing more infuriating than losing an item to another bidder for a few pounds. But having marked your catalogue with the maximum figure, or figures you are prepared to bid, stick to it on the day, as auction fever can make some people bid far more than they ever intended, only to regret it bitterly afterwards.

Even the regular buyer can fall into this trap.

On the day of the sale, arrive early so that you can take a seat where the auctioneer can see you easily. When the auction does start, you will find that the bidding will go very quickly on desirable items. But remain calm. The auctioneer who knows all the regulars will recognise the novice bidder, and once you have started bidding he will see that you are not left out of the running, by giving you an enquiring look when a bid has been made against you.

Sometimes an item will fail to reach its reserve – the figure that the auctioneer and his client have agreed is the lowest price the item may be allowed to be sold. This often puts the auctioneer in the difficult position of having only one bidder whose bid has stopped below the reserve. His only way out of this situation is to make 'bids off the wall', in which he acts for his client by accepting bids from imaginary people, in the hope of bringing his solitary bidder up to the reserve figure. If this fails, the item is then bought in by the auctioneer for his client. This practice is a perfectly acceptable and legitimate one.

If no reserve figure has been placed on an item, you could well get yourself a modest bargain if it is something in which the dealers are not interested in acquiring.

If the hammer falls on your bid, you will have to give your name and address to the auctioneer's assistant. Afterwards, all that is left for you to do is to go back later and pay for and collect your prize.

If you are unable, or do not want to attend the sale, you can make a bid by filling in a slip beforehand, obtainable at the auction rooms, in which you state the amount you are prepared to pay for a certain item. You can then phone in several hours after the auction to enquire if your bid has been accepted.

A final word on the business of buying at an auction, or anywhere else, for that matter. Before committing yourself in buying anything, always remember the legal principle, *caveat emptor* – let the buyer beware. Which is why it is so important to attend those viewing sessions.

GONE TO THAT GENTLEMAN FOR TEN THOUSAND POUNDS!

"Ten Frenchmen for one English prisoner," was Napoleon's answer, when the question of exchanging prisoners was put before him. Not unnaturally, this was a condition the British government was not prepared to accept, and the result was that thousands of French sailors and soldiers who had served the Emperor well, were condemned to sit out the war in places like Edinburgh Castle or in one of the prisons such as Dartmoor, which was built in 1809, solely for the purpose of housing French prisoners.

But the prisoners were fortunate in one respect. As well as providing them with food and clothing, the British government allowed them to while away the hours making articles for sale outside the prison to pay for such luxuries as tobacco and extra food. But having gone that far, the government stopped short at providing them with any materials.

Undaunted, the prisoners improvised using bones that had either been left on their dinner plates or scrounged from the kitchens. Human hair, pieces of wood and straw were a few of the other basic materials they used to create an amazingly wide range of small objects, which were often so superbly crafted that the prison guards had no difficulty in selling them outside for their charges. That many of them were so well made was largely due to the fact that many of the prisoners were craftsmen in their own right.

It might be thought that as prisoners they would have been greatly exploited, both by the guards and their patrons outside the prison walls. But generally speaking this does not seem to have been the case, as many of them are recorded as having received high prices for their work. One French prisoner who had made a model ship almost entirely from bone, was paid a hundred pounds for his model — a very large sum of money for those days. Many others are known to have built themselves up a nice nest egg for the future, when they finally ended their captivity.

It is with the model ships that we see the ultimate expression of this prison craft. Many of them were commissioned by wealthy patrons, and one can understand why when one examines them, as the very best of them are marvels of ingenuity, with every part working, right down to their tiny brass guns that could run out.

Unhappily, modern copies have been made of some of these ships and sold as originals, which means that anyone coming across a

prisoner of war model ship should be very careful before reaching for their cheque book.

The work of the prisoners who specialised in making knick-knacks out of straw became so popular that the straw plaiting industry was moved to complain to the government, who responded by ordering that any straw found in a prisoner's cell should be confiscated. But although periodical raids were made on the cells, they were still made.

It is generally assumed that the prisoner of war crafts were done only by the French prisoners. But this was very far from being the case. After the beginning of the War of Independence, American prisoners began to arrive at the English prisons, where they soon proved themselves to be just as skilled as their French counterparts in making articles for sale outside, particularly with their ship models. But for some reason their work seems to be less available — perhaps because much of it was passed off as the French prisoner work, which seems to be held in higher regard.

Any detailed information on prisoner of war work is not easy to come by, and a large number of books dealing with general antiques do not even cover the subject. However, some fine collections are to be seen in museums, particularly at the Peterborough museum and at the Science Museum in London, and at the Royal Maritime Museum at Greenwich, who both house a number of model ships.

BEAUTY FROM OLD BONES

Above left: An early 19th century French prisoner of war Spinning Jenny, fully articulated.

Above right: An early 19th century wash-stand in bone, with drawer to base.

Photographs: Courtesy of **King & Chasemore, (Pulborough).**

BLUE-EYED BABIES

'I once had a sweet little doll, dears,
   The prettiest doll in the world:
   Her cheeks were so red and white, dears,
And her hair so charmingly curled.'

Those words, written by Charles Kingsley in *The Water Babies,* published in 1863, must have struck a responsive chord in many a young girlish heart in England, where dolls had now become the rage since the Montanaris, a family of doll makers, had exhibited their range of wax dolls at the Great Exhibition of 1851.

The Montanari dolls were prohibitively expensive for those days, costing more than five pounds for an undressed model. There was, however, no shortage of buyers.

Almost as famous a family of doll makers during that period was the Pierotti family, who supplied the London toyshops of Hamleys with dolls right up to 1930.

But although the Pierotti family had been making dolls in England since the 1780's, the baby doll as we understand it, did not exist in England or any other country unti 1825, when Germany began to export a new type of doll made of flesh coloured papier mâché, dipped in wax solution to give an impression of human skin.

Previously, the dolls had been made in the shape of a woman, and were very crude affairs, with the head moulded in papier mâché, to which a stuffed body was attached.

That dolls that existed at all during that period is rather surprising, when one realises that a child unfortunate enough to have been born in the 18th century was expected to become an adult as soon as it was out of baby clothes, and was therefore encouraged to put away childish things as soon as possible.

The birth of the great Victorian middle class saw a change which paved the way to a new attitude to children. Instead of being treated with indifference, they were now seen as 'little angels', who, in time, would grow up in the image of their mothers, and, in turn, would become mothers themselves. What better toy, then, for a little girl, than a baby doll on which she could indulge her latent maternal instincts?

It was the Victorian middle class who promoted the sale of the doll, when they decided it was the ideal toy with which their little girls could develop their latent maternal instincts.

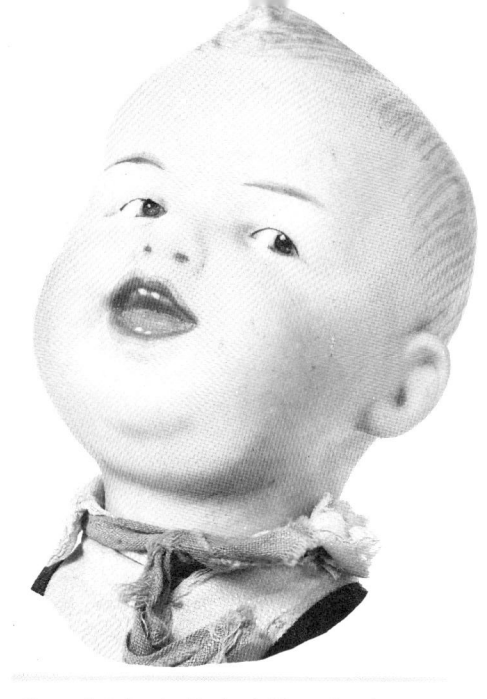

Suddenly faced with an ever-increasing demand for dolls, the manufacturers began supplying them in large quantities.

The earlier dolls such as the German 'Biedermeir' dolls of the 1840s, with their rigid bodies and painted wooden limbs began to be replaced by dolls made of wax or china, and were not only well dressed, but also supplied with parasols, gloves, and sometimes a lace shawl.

Although England had now become the leader in their manufacture, Germany was also still making dolls in large numbers. They arrived in England with a hole in the crown, which was there for the very good reason that its reduced weight led to a lower tariff charge. On its arrival, the hole was generally closed up with some composition, such as cardboard, and hidden under a wig.

By the 1860s, the English doll makers were routed for a while by the appearance of the French 'Fashion Dolls', whose bodies were made from stitched kid and then dressed in elaborate clothes that reflected the latest styles of the French fashion houses. Often supplied with furs and jewellery, they represent the ultimate in luxury toys for those who could afford them. But again, as in the case of the Montanari dolls, there was no lack of buyers.

At the other end of the scale in this country, there was the popular stuffed doll, the wooden Dutch doll, with its painted head and joints secured by tiny pegs, tiny dolls that cost only a farthing each, the indestructible rubber dolls made by Goodyear, and the black-faced golliwog.

The Americans contribution to the field in dolls were notably mechanical, and included the Goodwin clockwork walking doll, which pushed a three-wheeled vehicle, and a phonograph doll, patented by Edison in 1878. The doll was a marvel of ingenuity which sang nursery rhymes played on a little machine fitted inside the body. Other fine automata dolls were produced in France by the firms of Janeau and Bru, which are highly collectible —and expensive.

All of them represented various stages in the evolution of the doll, whose origins go back to remote antiquity.

Dolls were known in ancient Egypt, and were common in the days of early Greece and Rome. Cortez, the 16th century conqueror of Mexico, is said to have found the Aztec leader, Montezuma, and his court playing with elaborate dolls dug up from prehistoric Peruvian graves.

They were to be found among the African tribes, the Australian aborigines, the Red Indians, and the Esquimaux. More often than not, they were made in the image of man. Some of them were ancestor images, others acted as lucky charms, and a third group were supposed to possess magical powers.

It is not until we reach the medieval period in Europe that dolls made in wood or clay and shaped in the image of a woman, began to appear. Even then they were referred to as children's babies, rather than dolls, a word that came into being sometime after 1750, and was taken from the Norse word *daul* (woman).

The wooden head replaced by the china head, hair marked by modelling or painted on

Above. A Gebruder Heubach bisque head character doll with moulded painted hair, sideways glancing intaglio blue eyes, open/close mouth with moulded teeth and dressed composition body.

Left. A Schoenau and Hoffmeister bisque Oriental doll with mohair wig, fixed eyes, open mouth with upper teeth and jointed composition body, dressed in national costume.

Below. A Lenci Fabric Boy Doll with brown wig and painted brown eyes. **Right.** A Lenci Fabric Girl Doll, with blonde wig and pierced ears with earrings. The patchwork is in pink and white, with matching shoes.

replaced by flax, mohair and even real hair, eyes that could open and close, the doll that could speak and walk, have all played their part in the evolution of the doll which today can dance, drink from a bottle, have a nappy rash and hair that actually grows.

But despite all the tremendous expertise which has been put into the development of the modern doll, it is still highly debatable that they have more to offer a child than those famous china dolls of the 19th century.

Today, some of those 19th century dolls fetch staggering prices in the auction rooms, with sums being paid for them well in excess of £2,000.

Mechanical dolls or dolls made in the likeness of historical figures can fetch even higher prices.

On the other hand, even if you do have to pay a high price for a doll, it can still represent a good investment if you buy wisely. It is all too easy, though, to make a costly mistake. It is therefore well worth taking the trouble to acquire some specialised knowledge, either by reading some books on the subject, or by visiting museums. Nearly all of them have at least a small collection of dolls. The London Museum, for an instance, has a fine collection of Queen Victoria's dolls. They represent real people whom she had met, or an important stage actress of the age. Considering the money that was available, they are not very good examples of the dolls being made at that time, but they are still well worth studying.

If you buy in auction, it is very important to examine them on a viewing day before the actual auction to see if they have been repaired or been badly damaged. The cracking of a wax surface is a common flaw in many wax dolls on the market, and something to be watched for.

Although no auction room would knowingly sell you a fake, they are around, so if you're buying from a dealer or privately, be sure you know what you are about. If you should start collecting dolls, they should be under glass. Otherwise moths and moisture could wreak havoc with them.

WHERE TO BUY

Kay Desmonde. 17 Kensington Church Street, London W8.
The Singing Tree, 69 New King's Road, London SW6.
Anthea Knowles Rare Toys and Fine Dolls, 42 Colebrooke Road, London N1.
Yesterday Child, 24 The Mall, Camden Passage, London N1.
Dolls and Toys of Yesteryear, Bow House Antiques, 3-4 Faulkner Square, Charnham Street, Hungerford, Berks.
Lilian Middleton's Antique Dolls Shop, Sheep Street, Stow-on-the-Wold, Glos.

MUSEUMS

London: London Museum (housing Queen Mary's collection of dolls.
Bethnal Green Museum.
Horniman Museum, Dulwich.
Edinburgh: Museum of Childhood.
Manchester: Queen's Park Art Gallery.
Norwich: Stranger's Hall.
Rottingdean: Toy Museum.
Worthing: Museum and Art Gallery.
York: Castle Museum.

BOOKS

Dolls by John Noble
Collector's History of Dolls by C. Eileen King.

Left: A papier mâché doll dressed as a Highlander of the 72nd Foot, and a papier mâché doll dressed as a guard. Phillips.

Right. A Kammer and Reinhardt bisque head doll, with a brown wig and sleeping brown eyes, and a jointed composition body.

Left: An early doll made from mixed materials.

-PARIAN-

For twenty five years Parian ware was bought by everyone because it looked expensive, which it wasn't. Then it went out of fashion...

POPULAR PORCELAIN

Although the Minton porcelain factory claimed at one time that it was the first to produce Parian ware, it is now generally accepted that the Copeland factory at Stoke on Trent, was the first to market it. The invention of a Derby figure maker named Mountford, who had come to work for Copeland, it was given its name because of its resemblance to Parian marble from the Greek island of Paros, which was famous in ancient times for the wonder of its sculpture.

Mountford found that by mixing two parts of felstar with one part of kaolin, he could produce a form of porcelain that could be fired at the unglazed or biscuit stage, so that it assumed a dull sheen that made it look like Parian marble. It was first marketed by Copeland in 1844, and the process was soon also adopted by Wedgewood and Minton, and later by the Worcester factory. To begin with, what was produced mostly was statuary porcelain of such famous figures as Sir Walter Scott, William Shakespeare and the Duke of Wellington. Busts of the Royal family were particularly popular, as were neo-classical figures. The Victorian love of sentimentality was also much in evidence with such figures as *Dancing Girl Reposing,* and *Lesbia,* a bust of a girl with a sparrow nesting on her shoulder. Another popular piece was *The Veiled Bride,* made by Copeland in 1861. The Crystal Palace Art Union described it with some truth as ''a work of great beauty and wonderously executed.''

The growing popularity of Parian ware was given a boost when the Art Union of London decided that the oil paintings they were giving away in their yearly raffles to promote art, were far too valuable a prize to be given away. Instead, they began giving away Parian pieces, which they mostly produced themselves. One of their more famous pieces was *Narcissus,* of which fifty copies were made. It is not recorded how the lottery winners felt about being fobbed off with a mass produced piece of porcelain, when other previous winners had won an oil painting, which in most cases had been shown at the Royal Academy first.

For twenty five years, an enormous quantity of busts, statuettes and various pieces were produced by nearly every china factory in the country. A number of them, including Copeland, employed a number of distinguished sculptors of the day to model pieces for them. The reproduction of these sculptors was greatly helped by the pantograph, the invention of a sculptor named Benjamin Cheverton, which made it possible to scale down accurately and very quickly a full sized figure to whatever size it was needed.

Copeland's Parian bust of 'The Veiled Bride',
after an original sculpture by Raphael Monti.
Courtesy of Sotherby's.

The great merit of Parian ware for many was that it was inexpensive, and well in the range of most people's pockets. As it continued to increase in popularity, manufacturers turned their eyes to producing it in other forms for a mass market. Dessert services, butter dishes and jugs — often issued as a set of three jugs of varying sizes — began to appear. To some degree it was to sound the death knell for Parian ware.

The major factories, however, still continued to produce fine examples of Parian ware. Minton, who had displayed at the Great Exhibition of 1851, no less than forty six Parian figures, issued some very nice jugs and vases, which have become popular with modern collectors. A newcomer to the scene was the Beleek factory in County Fermanagh, Ireland, who began marketing Parian ware that was so delicately made as to make many other pieces of Parian seem positively crude by comparison.

The factory of Robinson and Leadbetter, which probably produced more Parian ware than any other factory, helped to popularise it in America, when they started to ship it there in large quantities. This encouraged the American porcelain factories to produce their own Parian ware, notably the Bennington factory at Vermont in New England, who produced a fine range of Parian figures, including a charming figure of Red Riding Hood, a copy of which now resides in the Metropolitan Museum of Art in New York.

Although it was still being collected towards the end of the 19th century, the vogue for collecting it began to die out — due mainly to the large quantities of shoddy pieces on the market.

Although the factory of Beleek still continues to produce Parian ware, it is something that belongs very much to the Victorian age, which has meant that it has become very collectable. If you happen to see a piece you fancy yourself, don't be discouraged from buying it because it looks dirty. Some warm water, a soft cloth and some washing up liquid will bring it up as good as new.

MUSEUMS
London: British Museum, Victoria and Albert Museum.
Stoke on Trent: City Museum and Art Gallery.
Worcester: Dyson Perrins Museum of Worcester Porcelain.

BOOKS
Victorian Porcelain by G . Godden, 1961.
Victorian Pottery and Porcelain by G. Bernard Hughes, 1959.
For best buys: Try the Antique Markets, especially Antiquarius, 135 Kings Road, London.

1

2

5

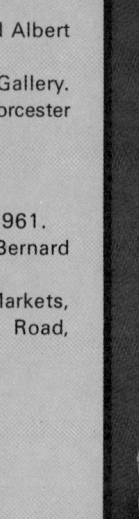

3

4

6

7

1. The cricketer W.G. Grace.

2. A classical figure and a chimney sweep.

3. Lady Godiva on Horseback.

4. A bust of General Gordon.

5. A set of Parian busts and busts.

6. Dorothea. A Minton Parian piece.

7. A Robinson and Leadbetter figure of Venus.

Pictures 1. 2. 3. 4. 6. Courtesy of Phillips.
5. 7. Courtesy of Sotherby's.

Photographs by Courtesy of:
The Priory Gallery – Cheltenham.

1. *Lady in Blue* by William Barribal 18" x 12"

2. *Sweet Roses* by Charles Edward Wilson
3. *The Young Anglers* by Thomas MacKay 8" x 11"
4. *The First Post* by Walter Langley 20" x 16"
5. *The Wheel-Barrow* by Miles Birket Foster
6. *A Country Lane* by Claude Strachan
7. *The Horse Fair* by John Atkinson 15" x 20"
8. *Haymaking* by Arthur Hopkins

WATERCOLOURS
the Joy of the Chase

There are a number of good reasons for collecting watercolours. You do not have to pay a fortune to acquire a reasonable collection, they provide an immediate visual pleasure to the eye for the owners and their visitors, they reflect – for better or worse – their owner's taste and personality in a way that no other antique can, and, unlike a piece of porcelain that can be smashed by a careless elbow or duster, they are unlikely to come to any harm if they are kept out of the sun.

With Victorian watercolours in particular, the collector leads a life of permanent adventure. Because the Victorians seem to have been possessed with a fever for painting

6

7

8

watercolours, we have been left with a staggering legacy of thousands upon thousands of their watercolours, which has meant that there is hardly a town in the whole of Britain which hasn't some antique shop with a few Victorian watercolours on its walls. It is only fair to add that most of them are not worth a second look.

The picture galleries that also abound throughout Britain are something else again. Nearly all of them carry a large stock of good quality watercolours, and most of them are owned by men and women from other walks of life, who have opened a gallery because they love watercolours.

By all means continue browsing through the antique shops. After all, someone did find a Dürer (admittedly an oil) stuck on a nail in a junk shop. But if you're going seriously into collecting watercolours, it is probably in your best interests to put yourself in the hands of one of these galleries. You will find them helpful and only too happy to show you their stock, and you will probably do better with them price-wise than you would in most auction rooms, where you will find yourself saddled with the 10% Buyer's Premium tacked on the price. All this, though, applies more to your regional Picture Gallery than some of the major London galleries, where prices tend to match the overheads.

Where to Buy

Peter Arnold,
3 Knolls Close,
Wingrave,
Aylesbury, **Bucks.**

Bourne Gallery,
Lesbourne Road,
Reigate, **Surrey.**

Barronfield Gallery,
47 Friargate, **Preston.**

Cambridge Fine Art,
33 Church Street,
Little Shelford,
Cambridge.

Marks Wood Gallery,
Great Barfield,
Nr. Baintree, **Essex.**

The Priory Gallery,
Station Road,
Bishop's Cleeve,
Cheltenham.

Leverington Hall
Gallery, Leverington,
Wisbech, **Cambs.**

Wharfedale Galleries,
30 Main Street,
Burley in Wharfedale,
Nr. Ilkley,
West Yorkshire.

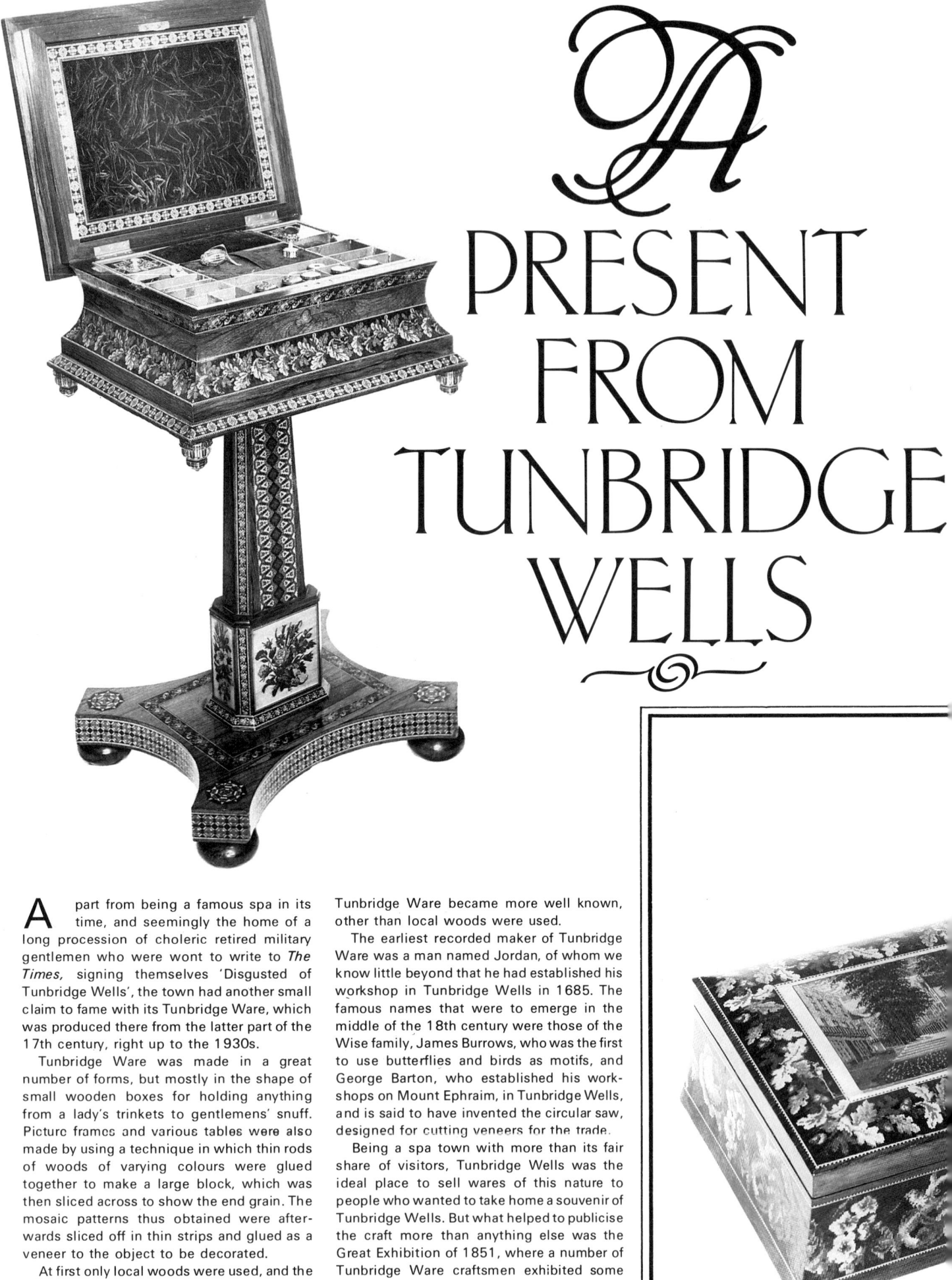

A PRESENT FROM TUNBRIDGE WELLS

A part from being a famous spa in its time, and seemingly the home of a long procession of choleric retired military gentlemen who were wont to write to *The Times,* signing themselves 'Disgusted of Tunbridge Wells', the town had another small claim to fame with its Tunbridge Ware, which was produced there from the latter part of the 17th century, right up to the 1930s.

Tunbridge Ware was made in a great number of forms, but mostly in the shape of small wooden boxes for holding anything from a lady's trinkets to gentlemens' snuff. Picture frames and various tables were also made by using a technique in which thin rods of woods of varying colours were glued together to make a large block, which was then sliced across to show the end grain. The mosaic patterns thus obtained were afterwards sliced off in thin strips and glued as a veneer to the object to be decorated.

At first only local woods were used, and the craftsmen involved took great pride in advertising that no artificial dyes were used. Experiments were often undertaken to find new ways of naturally dying the wood. It was found, for an instance, that minerals in the local water dyed white woods, after a long soaking, to greys and blues. Later, when Tunbridge Ware became more well known, other than local woods were used.

The earliest recorded maker of Tunbridge Ware was a man named Jordan, of whom we know little beyond that he had established his workshop in Tunbridge Wells in 1685. The famous names that were to emerge in the middle of the 18th century were those of the Wise family, James Burrows, who was the first to use butterflies and birds as motifs, and George Barton, who established his workshops on Mount Ephraim, in Tunbridge Wells, and is said to have invented the circular saw, designed for cutting veneers for the trade.

Being a spa town with more than its fair share of visitors, Tunbridge Wells was the ideal place to sell wares of this nature to people who wanted to take home a souvenir of Tunbridge Wells. But what helped to publicise the craft more than anything else was the Great Exhibition of 1851, where a number of Tunbridge Ware craftsmen exhibited some truly magnificent pieces.

The craft of making Tunbridge Ware died out briefly in 1899, but was revived again in the 1920s, and was carried on right into the 1930s, notably by Thomas Green of Rye, Sussex, who could claim to be the very last practitioner of this unusual craft.

Left hand page: A needlework box on a pedestal.
Above: A jewel cabinet made by George Wise Jr.
Left: A group of Tunbridge Ware boxes; including one showing a view of the Pantiles.
Pictures courtesy of Tunbridge Wells Museum.

MUSEUMS

LONDON Bethnal Green Museum.

MAIDSTONE Borough Museum & Art Gallery.

TUNBRIDGE WELLS Municipal Museum, housed in the public library.

BOOKS

Tunbridge and Scottish Woodware by Edward and Eva Pinto.

Mansions, Men and Tunbridge Ware by Ethel Younghusband.

NOTE Examples of Tunbridge Ware can generally be found in most of the antique markets.

a flutter of
FANS

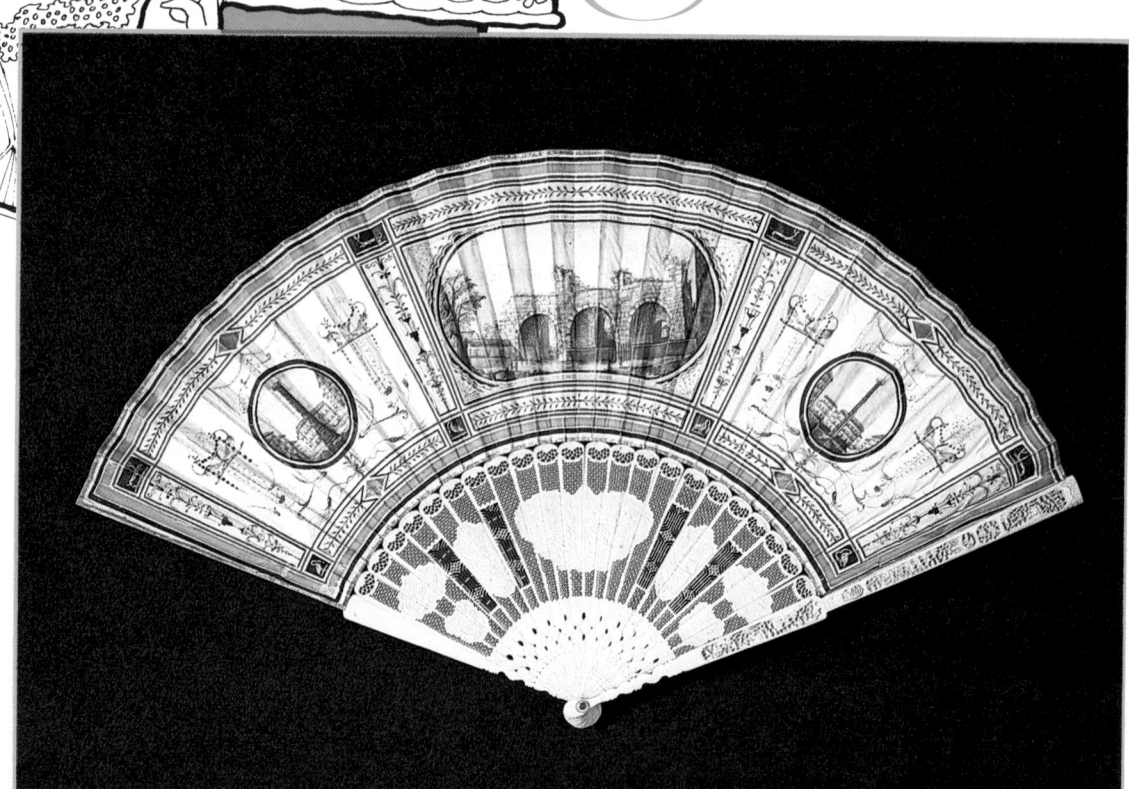

Right. A late 18th Century
Italian fan with views of
Rome and Pompeian
decoration.

Below. A late 18th
Century fan with a
coloured stipple engraving
of Venus nursing Cupid,
with roundels of neo-
classical maidens.

MUSEUMS
London: Victoria and
Albert Museum.
Aylesbury: Weddeston
Manor.
Bath: Museum of
Costume.
Birmingham: City
Museum.
Glasgow: Art Gallery
and Museum.
Hereford: City Museum
and Art Gallery.
Newcastle: Laing
Museum.
Southampton: Tudor
House (Franks
Collection).
York: Castle Museum.

The 18th century was the heyday of the fan, particularly the folding fan, which was originally made in Japan and exported to China. To begin with, most of the fans came from France, and were exquisitely made, often with scenes on them which had been painted by such famous artists as Watteau and Boucher. Many of them were heavily ornamented, with the sticks made out of mother of pearl or ivory, and printed on a fine vellum called 'chicken skin'. But when the French Revolution came, fans were considered an effete luxury of the nobility, and the making of them almost died out until more settled times.

The fact that there are so many English fans still available to the collector, we owe to some degree ot the large exhibition of fans that was held in the South Kensington Museum in 1870, which led to an enormous demand for fans the manufacturers were not slow to meet.

The subjects used on the new fans varied greatly. There were religious fans, fans for the theatre goer, showing the seats or boxes taken by important subscribers to a theatre, and there were mourning fans, fortune telling fans, and even conversation fans.

Queen Victoria, who seems to have collected *everything,* including a lot of items that were the epitome of bad taste, also collected fans. She was particularly fond of Dutch fans, decorated by heraldic paintings in a process called "Vernis Martin", after the inventor of a colourless lac varnish.

Fortunately for us many attactive fans were still produced that equalled anything that had been made in pre-revolutionary France.

Left. A late 18th Century Chinese fan.

Below. A mid-19th Century Chinese fan.

PHILLIPS

WHERE TO BUY
Mrs Brenda Gunn,
Stall N 13, Antiquarius
Market, Chelsea,
London.
Fantiques 18-20 Hill
Avenue, Amersham,
Bucks.
Arca 351 Grays
Antique Market, 58
Davies St, London

BOOKS
Collector's History of
Fans by Nancy
Armstrong.
The Fan by Mary
Gostelow.
The Collector's Guide
to Fans by Bertha de
Vere Green.
More Small
Decorative Antiques
(English Fans) Therle
Hughes.

Papier Mâché

PLEASURE FROM PULPED PAPER

There was a time when **everything** seemed to be made in papier mâché — including a replica of H.M.V.'s famous dog, Nipper, seen bottom left.

Although the art of making papier mâché had long been practised in the East, it was not until the early part of the 18th century that the French started to produce it on a large scale. When a quantity of papier mâché items were imported into Germany, the attracted the attention of Frederick the Great, who was so taken with them that he established a factory for its production in Berlin in 1765.

He was still rather late in the field as papier mâché was being produced in England as early as 1735. But it was Henry Clay, a Birmingham manufacturer, who was to lead the way in its production. In 1722, he patented a process in which many layers of paper were glued together and then heated and dried at 100°F, after each layer had been applied. It was a long and arduous process in which ten layers of paper had to be applied to make a simple tea tray. And this was only the beginning of the process, which then called upon the skills of an artist, who painted decorative flower pictures on the object before several applications of varnish were applied.

The decorative use of mother of pearl came later, when a Birmingham firm called Jennens and Bettridge, obtained a patent in 1825, for making certain improvements in preparing and working pearl shell in various forms and applying it to ornamental uses in the manufacture of paper and other wares.

And what a tedious process it was, involving the filing and grinding and rubbing with a pumice, pieces of flat shell until they were reduced to a thickness of 100 of an inch. After the shell had been thus thinned, it was cut to the required design and then attached by adhesives. After that there was still the laying of coat after coat of varnish and rubbing the surface with a leather until everything was on

Top. *Two fans painted with scenes of Osborne House and Ryde, Isle of Wight.*

Phillips.

Top. Tray decorated in gilt
Above. Tray with raised chinoiserie design.
PHILLIPS

the same level. Considering the amount of work involved in making some of the pieces of papier mâché, it is surprising that much of it can still be bought at a reasonable price.

The most popular colour used for japanning was black, but items were also produced in crimson and green. When Price Albert died, some manufacturers went a stage further and produced articles in which mauve and grey paints were used, together with mother of pearl.

Papier mâché was actually produced by a number of processes involving the use of pulped paper or rags, but the common factor with all them was their attractive japanned surfaces which appealed to people from all walks of life. With the manufacturers producing everything from buttons to furniture in papier mâché, it was hardly surprising that a number of them became wealthy, especially Henry Clay, who opened a thriving business in Bedford Street, in London, which was supplied by his Birmingham factory, where he employed more than 600 people.

But the keen interest shown in papier mâché, suddenly waned in the last quarter of the 19th century, when the public decided that it was vulgar and worthless. Time has proved them wrong.

Top. Nest of tables with painted scenes circa 1860, and work table with mother of pearl top, circa 1850.
Right. 'Jacobsen' style chair, circa 1850.
Below. Bedstead with lacquered brass mounts and original canopy, circa 1850.
The Antique Dealer and Collector's Guide.

MUSEUMS

London: Victoria and Albert Museum
Birmingham City Museum and Art Gallery
Cardiff: The National Museum of Wales.
Wolverhampton: Municipal Art Gallery, Bantock House.

BOOKS

English Papier Mâché of the Georgian and Victorian Periods by Shirley Spaulding, De Voe.
English Papier Mâché—It's Origin, Development and Decline, by George Dickenson.

A typical bears' grease pot lid.
Courtesy **Phillips**.

The Victorians knew as well as us the value of an eye-catching piece of packaging as a selling aid to their wares, and one of the most attractive ideas ever to come into being during that period was the use of multi-coloured transfer prints on pot lids, which was successfully commercialised by Felix Pratt, after it had been invented by one of his employees named Jesse Austin who had

spent three years perfecting the process.

That it was possible at all was due to George Baxter, who had invented a process of producing colour prints by using oil based inks and wooden blocks, one for each colour.

But there was a problem when it came to producing the pot lids. Baxter had taken out a patent protecting his idea. But, somewhat unscrupulously, some people might think,

Austin got round the problem by reversing Baxter's process in which the outline was printed first. Austin printed the colour plates first and then printed the outline last.

From a marketing point of view, Pratt's pot lids came out just at the right time, in the 1840's. An already flourishing trade had already begun with the selling of small pots containing a form of solidified brilliantine made from the fat of polar and grizzly bears. This was called, understandably, 'bears' grease', which men had begun using as a hair fixative since the government decided to tax the special dusting powder they had previously used on their wigs and hair.

The bears' grease pot lids had previously been printed only in black, and were generally thrown away after they had been emptied. After they had begun to appear with multi-coloured lids, they became collectors' pieces, which were often framed in black ebony and placed on the wall.

The success of Pratt's pot lids led to other manufacturers using the idea to sell their wares. Tatnall and Son, and S. Bangor, who were both fish paste manufacturers, started commissioning lids with views of Pegwell Bay, Ramsgate and Margate, and others followed suit, covering a large range of products, including 'Old Civet Cat Cold Cream'. One cannot help wondering what *that* smelled like.

A number of Staffordshire potteries produced pot lids, but none of them really equalled those made by Jesse Austin, who continued to design them for Pratt until his death, barring one year when he left Pratt, presumably over a quarrel, only to return. The range of subjects, as with Stevengraphs, was enormous. It has been estimated that there were more than three hundred designs made – most of them coming from Pratt's factory. Austin died in 1879, and soon afterwards the popularity of the pot lid waned, though they were still being produced until the end of the century, when the factory was sold, shortly after Pratt's death in 1894, at the age of eighty.

It is generally considered that the lids made after Austin's death were not up to the standard of those printed prior to 1880. But this is somewhat unfair to the Pratt factory, which continued to produce quite a large number of quality lids right up to the end.

What the collector has more cause to worry about is the large number of reproductions that were made until quite recent times. These would not deceive an expert, but a novice buyer could be fooled. The thing to look for is a certain coarseness in the design which has been printed on a flat top in rather pale colours. Lids that have been framed should also be looked on with a certain amount of suspicion as the frame can hide a number of tell-tale clues as to its authenticity.

The early potlids can often be identified because of the fine crazing that appears on them. Not that this has deterred the forger from putting on his own crazing, though this can generally be spotted by a keen eye looking for particularly large crazing, which indicates that a forger has been at work.

As to the present day values of the lids, the best guide is Price Guide to Potlids, which is brought out annually by the Antique Collectors' Club at Woodbridge.

Above left: *The Faithful Shepherd.*
Right: *The Buffalo Hunt.*
Below left: *The Volunteers.*
Right: *Bear Hunting.*

Above: *Rare non Pratt lid from a Fry's chocolate paste pot.*

Left: *A Pegwell Bay fish paste pot lid.* **Right:** *Unique exhibition pot lid, New York 1853.*

SILVER~

Silver gilt Art Nouveau wash bowl, jug and soap dish. 1903.

decorative & domestic

Above, from left to right. A coffee pot by Paul de Lamerie. 1742. Rococo cup and cover. 1744.

Left: Viennese silver-gilt cornucopia inset with panels of lapis lazulu and cornelians. Circa 1870.

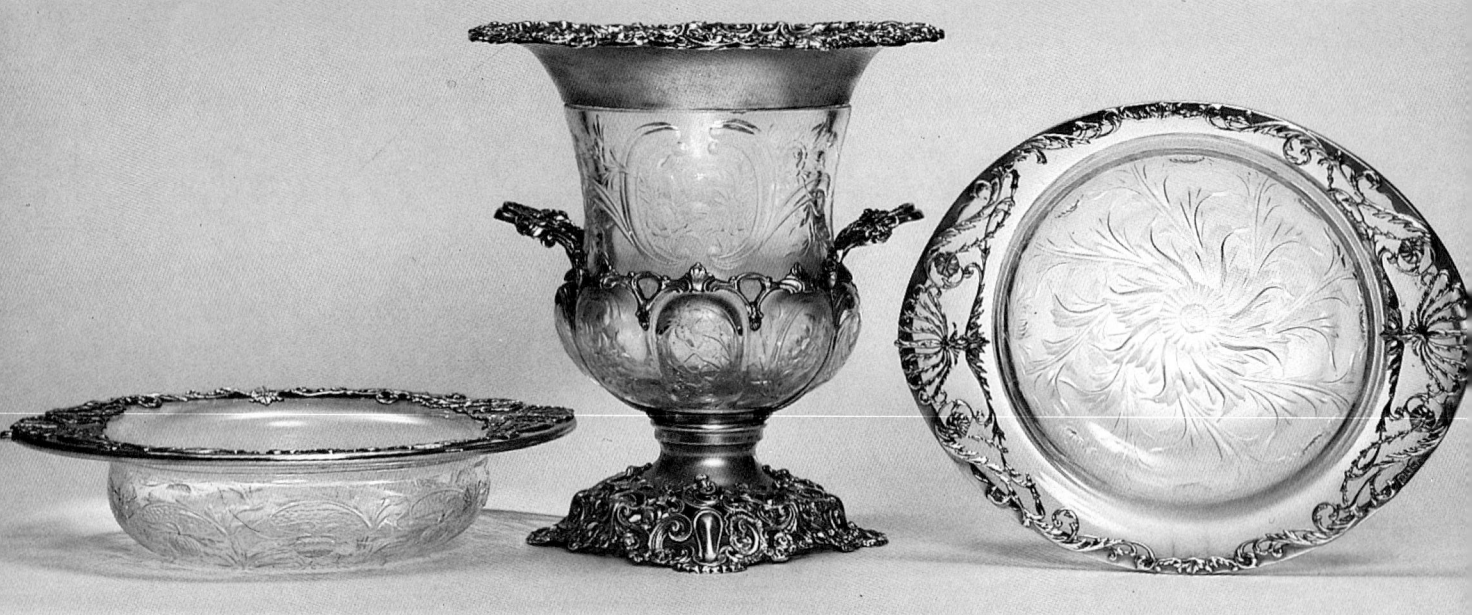

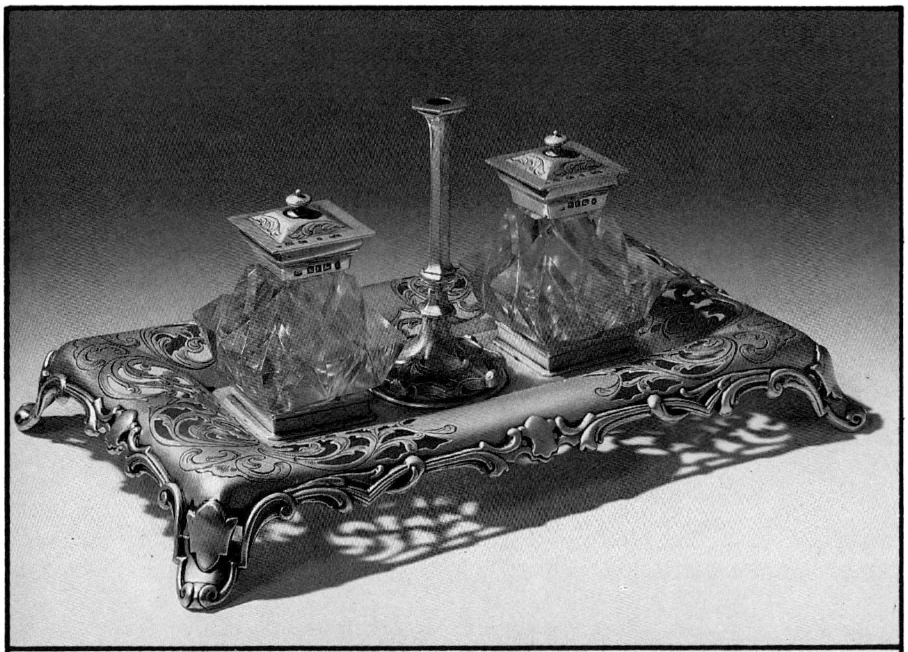

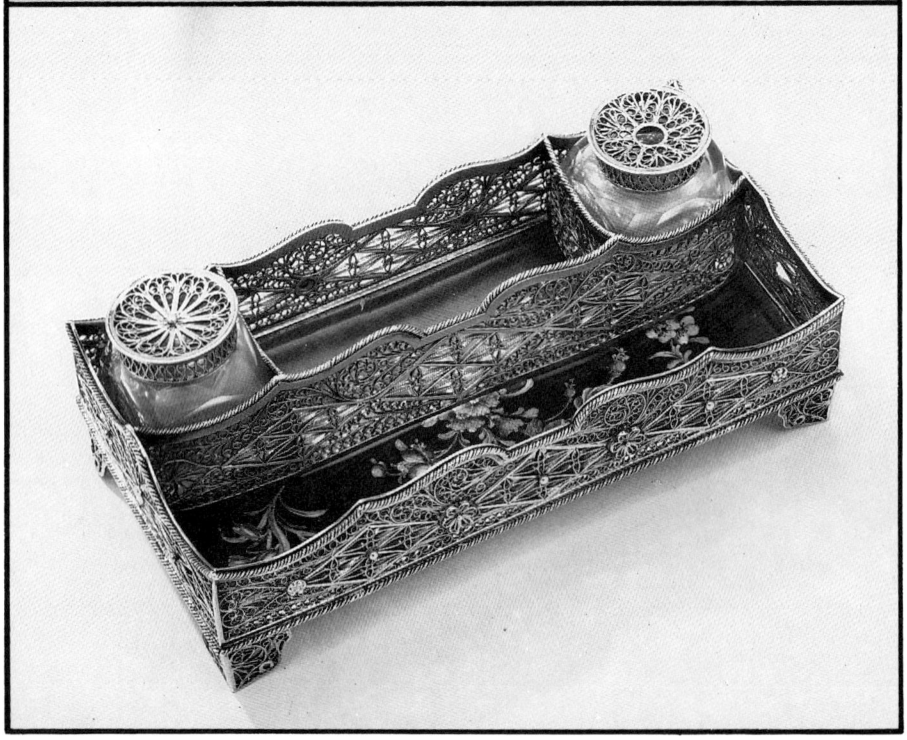

Above top to bottom: *Wine cooler and dessert dishes with silver mounts, 1910.* ***Left:*** *Victorian silver pierced inkstand, 1849.* ***Bottom left:*** *English filigree silver inkstand with Battersea enamel bottom. Circa 1760.*

Until this century, silver has always had two distinct functions. It could be made as coinage or crafted into ornaments which were either functional or decorative. It was used as coinage as far back as the days of Babylon, about 4500 BC, but as we are dealing with old silver, we are only concerned with that aspect of silver as far as it concerned how the word sterling came into being.

In approximately 1300, King John summoned to England a band of six German silversmiths from Hansa to create a standard for the silver coinage of the country. The Germans called themselves Easterlings, because they came from Eastern Europe, and the silver coinage they created was known by the same name until, by a statute of 1343, the first two letters were dropped from the word 'Easterling' and the word 'Sterling' came into being. The statute also established that the standard for silver should be 92.5 parts silver and 7.5 parts of base metal. When it had been tested by an assay office in London to see if it came up to the required standard, it was stamped with a leopard's head, which remains the London mark to the present day. Assay offices were later set up in other parts of the country. A further ordinance • was passed, ordering 'that each Master Goldsmith should have a mark to himself'. For anyone who is seriously interested in collecting old silver, it is essential to own a reference book which explains the whole system of hallmarks, both in this country and abroad, where the marks obviously vary from country to country.

The smithing of the first pieces of silver for decorative purposes in England was done by monks, who were primarily craftsmen, rather than men who had entered a monastary to escape from the world. Safe in the arms of the Church, which was the only body, apart from Royalty, who could afford to meet the prohibitive cost of gold and silver in those days, they were able to perfect their craft at leisure, often

George III silver drum tea caddy. Charles II silver porringer and cover 1660.
Right: *Victorian silver snuff box.*

spending months on one piece. By the time of the Middle Ages, goldsmithing (which embraced both the working of gold and silver) was ranked as one of the highest of the arts, and its craftsmen rewarded accordingly. By the time they had formed a guild, secular goldsmiths, who had served their apprenticeships under the monks, had begun producing what is now termed as domestic silver, designed especially for the wealthy who wished to give some visible sign of their wealth and power to their visitors.

From the thirteenth to the fifteenth century, England became more and more under the influence of foreign silversmiths. Although it was a period which saw the Renaissance style taking over, it was the French influence which dominated the scene until 1685, when Louis XIV suddenly revoked the Edict of Nantes, which had guaranteed for nearly a century, the freedom of worship, causing an immediate exodus of the Huguenots, who were to be responsible for the greatest flowering of the silversmith's work in England.

The greatest of all the Huguenot goldsmiths was undoubtedly Paul de Lamerie, who produced over a working span of nearly forty years in this country, some of the finest silver ever produced anywhere in the world. Lamerie worked in two styles, the severe, unornamented Queen Anne style, and the Huguenot style which drew on the rococo style of Juste-Aurele Meissonier, the designer, whose versions of the rococo sometimes verged on the grotesque. The Oxford Dictionary defines the word 'rococo' as 'meaningless decoration; tastelessly florid and ornate'. Although this can be applied to much that has been done in that style, it could never be applied to the work of Lamerie, who always kept it within the bounds of good taste.

In 1697, a new Act came into being, which laid down that from henceforth the content of fine silver should be increased to 95.85 parts of fine silver, and that pieces of this standard

were to have a new mark known as Britannia. This act had come about because of the habit of dishonest silversmiths accepting parcels of silver which included melted down coin clippings which lowered the value of the coin by as much as one-fifth of its proper weight. But the setting of a higher standard did not achieve its purpose, as silversmiths merely added pure silver to coin silver to increase the standard. In 1720 the Act was repealed, and silversmiths had the option of using either standard – a situation which exists to this day.

Fifty years after the Act was repealed, the rococo period ended and was replaced by a classical style in silver. Although the silver from this period lacks the grandeur of some of the better rococo pieces, its stark but elegant lines, so typical of the Georgian period, probably makes silver from this period more acceptable to modern eyes. The leading English silversmith of the period was Paul Storr, who registered his mark in 1792. Although he produced work in the rococo style, his best work was in the Adam style, in which he often drew his inspiration from Greek vases, or from the work of sculptor John Flaxman.

The arrival of the Victorian period saw a marked decline in the silversmith's craft, brought about in part by the invention of electro-plating by Elkington of Birmingham, who was able by this new process to make

inexpensive articles that closely resembled silver. But even worse, for the dedicated craftsman, was the sudden decline in taste throughout the whole of Europe: one has only to look at a catalogue for the Great Exhibition of 1851 to see just how badly standards had fallen in every field of the arts.

It was not until the Arts and Crafts Movement, which began in the last quarter of the nineteenth century, that we see standard improving again. Its founders, appalled by the age of mass production which had suddenly come upon them, set out to establish a situation where pure craftsmanship would once more be all important. The movement had a marked effect in many areas, and the new spirit was carried over to the age of Art Nouveau, in which we see once again silversmiths producing many beautiful pieces. (See article on Art Nouveau.)

Of all the fields of antique collecting, silver is the most exacting, calling as it does for some knowledge over a wide range of periods, styles and subjects which can range from enormous set pieces to a silver spoon. But it can also be one of the most exciting fields to explore, even for someone silver shopping on a budget. For those, there is the rewarding area of small silver, of which there seems to be an abundance at reasonable prices.

Photographs by courtesy of N. Bloom & Son.

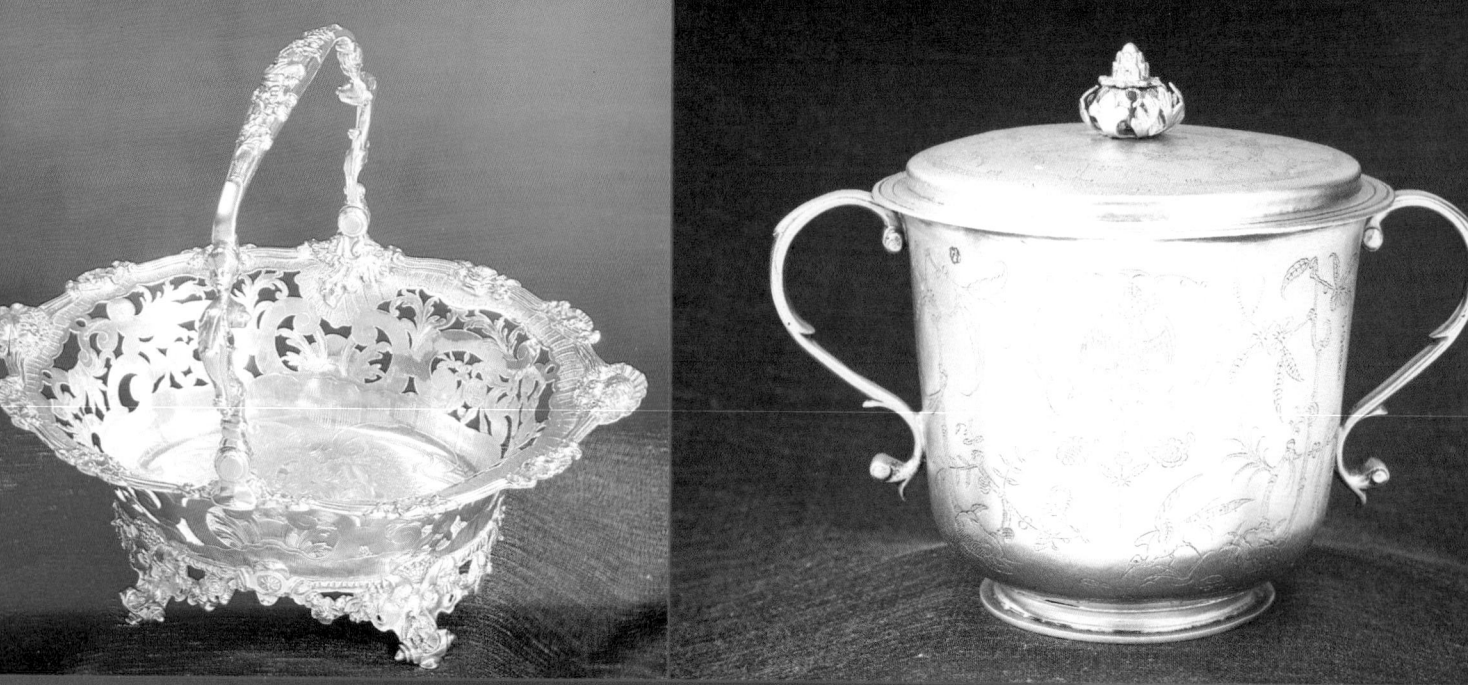

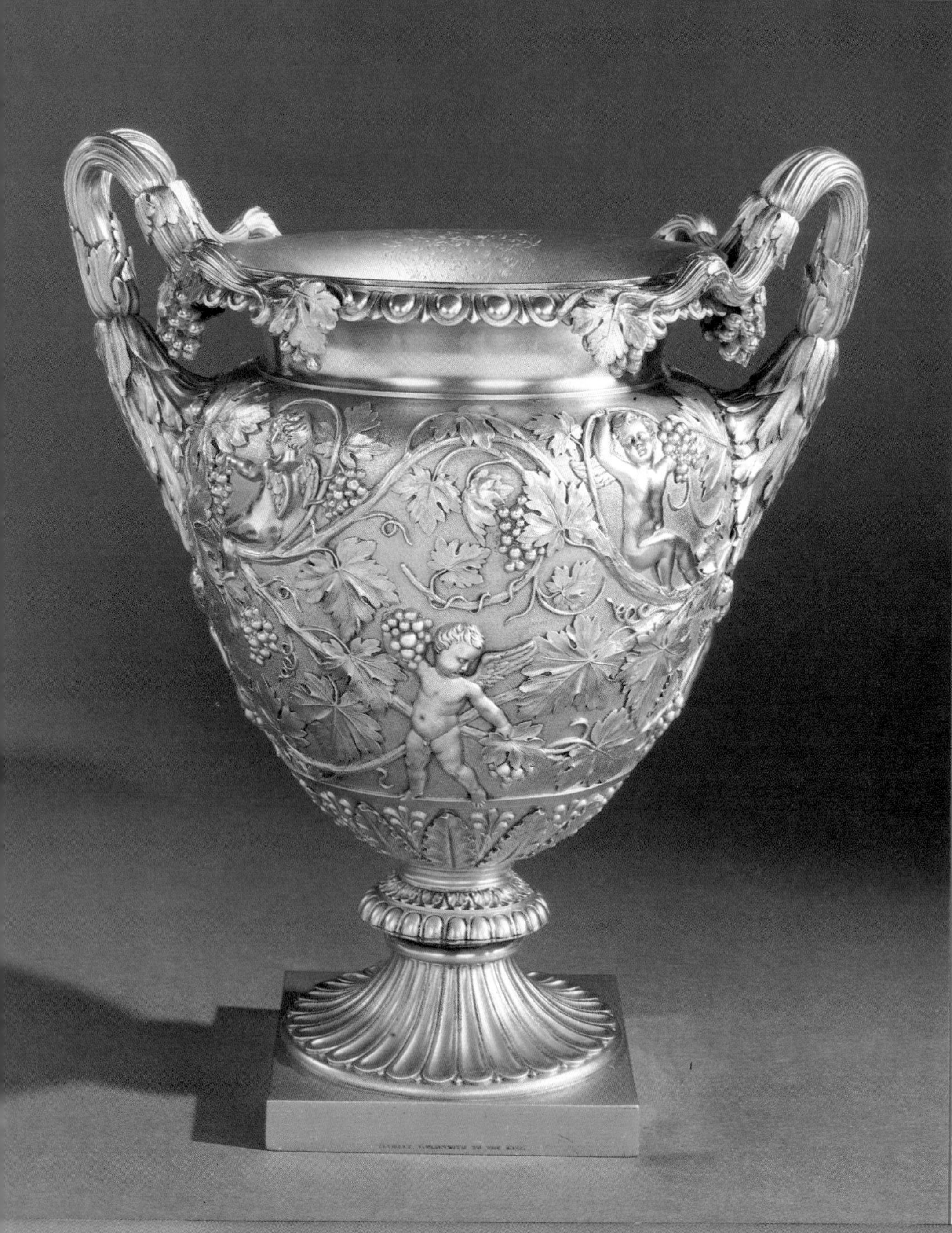

Above left: *Cake basket by Paul de Lamerie. 1745.*
Above: *Late 17th century silver-gilt Chinoiserie porringer and cover with original gilding. Engraved with the Spencer crest and motto for Charles, 3rd Duke of Marlborough.*
Left: *Large silver-gilt vase.*

Silver ~
Hall Marks

Assay marks are stamped on most genuine pieces of silver. They not only confirm the purity of the metal (the standard of which is laid down by law), they also indicate the place of assay, the date and the maker.

In Britain, the work of silversmiths has been regulated by Royal Ordinances and Acts of Parliament since the end of the 12th century. The record of the assay marks used before 1666, however, were lost in the Great Fire of London and the marks used from the 12th to the 17th century have been rediscovered over the years only after painstaking research.

Only a few cities were granted the privilege of marking silver. With the exception of London, which was permitted to mark silver from the 15th century, most did not receive their charters to do so until the 17th or 18th centuries. They were Chester, Dublin, Edinburgh, Exeter, Glasgow, Newcastle on Tyne, Norwich, Sheffield and York. A few minor guilds in towns including Cork, Greenock and Taunton were also allowed to mark their silver productions, which were mainly spoons.

London: Henry VIII (1509)

London: between 1679 and 1719

London (1836)

London (1952)

Birmingham (1800)

Chester (1850)

Dublin (1896)

Edinburgh (1786)

Exeter (1845)

Glasgow (1880)

Newcastle on Tyne (1870)

Norwich 1701)

Sheffield (1830)

York (1846)

The initial letter changes each year and goes through the alphabet (some offices go from A to U, leaving out J) and then the same letters of the alphabet are repeated again in a different type style. Note: The offices do not all start the alphabet in the same year.

The makers' names are shown either by their initials or their trademarks.

BOW
SPECIA

The history of the Bow porcelain factory is not so interesting as that of some of the other porcelain makers. Nor, for that matter, were the people attached to it so interesting as say, Nicholas Sprimont at the Chelsea factory or Dr. Wall at the Worcester factory, to say nothing of the famous Josiah Wedgewood. But it was, nevertheless, one of the most important of all the English porcelain companies throughout its existence from 1749 to 1775. It shared with Chelsea the honour of being the first porcelain factory in England, and it was certainly the very first to use calcined animal bones as one of the ingredients of its paste.

Despite the efforts of a large number of researchers, little is known of how the factory came into being, beyond the fact that in 1749, two men, an Edward Heylin, a merchant, and Thomas Frye, a painter, applied for a patent for producing a porcelain from the earth of the Cherokee nation living in North America, mixed with a large number of other substances, which were, it has been claimed since, quite unsuitable for making any form of porcelain. How Heylin and Frye came to know of this type of clay which the Indians referred to as 'unaker' remains a mystery to this day.

It has been alleged that the formula using this type of clay was a blind to confuse their competitors. If this was indeed the case, all that one can say is that everyone went to a lot of trouble and no little expense, to maintain the fiction, as the shipping of this clay went on for some twenty years.

However, a second patent was taken out by Frye alone in 1750, using calcined animal bones, and it was really from then that the history of Bow began.

The factory operated from Stratford-le-Bow and was initially financed by George Arnold, a rich Cheapside draper who died soon after-

Top left: A statue of General John Manners, Marquis of Granby. Circa 1760.
Left: Pair of figures of a lion and lioness, Circa 1750.
Right: An actor and Actress in Turkish dress, Circa 1750-52.
Courtesy Antique Dealer and Collectors Guide.

wards without having the chance to recoup his money, let alone have the pleasure of seeing the factory prosper. After his death, the factory came under the proprietorship of Crowther and Weatherby. But it was Frye who effectively ran it as its works manager until his death in 1762.

One of the first things to emerge from the factory was something known as New Canton, a glassy porcelain, not unlike Chelsea, decorated in the colour scheme of the *famille rose,* after the name given to a form of porcelain that. was produced in Canton, China, during the early part of the 18th century.

Bow's main aim was to produce wares which, while remaining a quality product were still inexpensive. Being a London based company that had the interests of the Londoner very much in mind, they produced a large number of statuettes and figures, many of them based on actors and actresses of the time in recognised roles. Another range depicted such national heroes as General Wolfe and the Marquis of Granby. Yet another range with general popular appeal, included harlequins, flower sellers and dancers, and figures representing the Four Seasons.

The early pieces of ware from Bow resem-

bled some of the early Lowestoft pieces, and were produced by a press moulding process which involved pressing the clay into the mould by hand. As all ceramics shrink during the initial firing, Bow attempted to get round the problem by making a square hole in the back to allow the air to escape.

As Chelsea and Bow were both based on the fringe of the metropolis, there was a considerable rivalry between the two factories. In fact, quite often their wares so closely resembled each others that it is often impossible to make an attribution to Bow, as their marks are not as clear as they should be.

LISTS · IN · FIGURES

BOW

However, a number of statuettes and figures are immediately identifiable — if you know something about Bow. The earliest figures are done in white and are in little flat stands which are rather crudely made compared to those on later figures. As with a number of other porcelain factories, they used a tree trunk or rocks or something of a similar nature, as a support, so that they could survive the ordeal of going through the furnace without being warped in the process.

A great deal of valuable information for identifying Bow china was supplied by the notebooks and diaries of John Bowcoate, the commercial manager and a traveller for the company. Even so, it is not always easy to identify Bow. Sometimes a piece can be identified by the minute bubbles that can be found on the base, caused when the glaze has gathered, often resulting in a greenish blue tinge. There is also a distinct lack of gilding on Bow wares, which are also quite heavy compared to wares from some other factories. Another way of identifying a Bow figure can sometimes be found with Bow's use of a daub of red on each cheek of a figure, which the factory found quite sufficient to colour the face. Chelsea at least stippled down the red to merge with the white. And of course there are always the museums where you can familiarize yourself with the general appearance of any of their lines.

Something that *is* easily recognisable to the expert is Bow's use of the Japanese Katiemon style, a process of painting in overglaze enamel colours which had been invented by Sakaida Katiemon in 1644, and was imitated by Chelsea and Worcester. The Bow versions, however, have a distinctive partridge pattern which is executed in a much more free style than those put out by their competitors.

The latter Bow pieces were sadly of an inferior quality. The porcelain was no longer of a fine quality, and often disfigured by black spots. The figures were not so well modelled and were often crudely painted — factors no doubt which helped to lead to the factory's demise when the surviving partner, Crowther, eventually went bankrupt. The factory was acquired by William Duesbury, who removed all the moulds and tools to his factory in Derby.

BOOKS

Bow, Chelsea and Derby Porcelain by W. Bemrose.
English Porcelain 1745-1850 by R.J. Charleston.
English Pottery and Porcelain by W.B. Honey.
Old English Porcelain by W.B. Honey.
Chelsea, Bow and Derby Porcelain by Frank Stoner.

MUSEUMS

London: The British Museum, London Museum, and the Victoria and Albert Museum.
Leicester: Museum and Art Gallery.

Left: *Figure of a Falconer. Circa 1757.*
Top right: *A pair of candlesticks, carrying mark of anchor and dagger. Circa 1760.*
Right: *Pair of rare Bow figures of a shepherd and shepherdess. Circa 1757.*
Pictures courtesy of the **Antique Porcelain Company** *London.*

WORCESTER
a favourite with the Gentry

The Worcester china factory has an almost unrivalled reputation for having produced porcelain of the highest quality from the middle of the 18th century until the present day. One uses the word 'almost' advisedly, as there was a period in its long history when it produced a range of porcelain notable for its bad taste.

This occurred after George III and Queen Charlotte had allowed them to style themselves as "China Manufacturers to their Majesties", following a visit they had made to the factory in 1788. Now calling themselves the Royal Porcelain Company, they suddenly found themselves being flooded with orders from the nobility and the gentry, which led them to producing needlessly elaborate dinner services in which taste was sacrificed on the altar of their clients' passion for the over-ornate. From a commercial point of view they were not wrong in doing so, as almost anyone with birth, rank or money, seems to have commissioned a dinner service from them.

These services, with their excessive gilding and giddy profusion of birds, flowers and fruit, often surrounding a coat of arms, were no longer produced after 1851.

It was, nevertheless, a period in which Worcester had added new dimensions to the art of pottery by their mastery of applying a fine glaze that never cracked, although fired at a fairly low temperature; they had introduced their famous and unrivalled China blue and white porcelain, and they had evolved a distinctive style of their own with their jugs, globular teapots, sauce boats and openwork baskets, and a large range of table ware which included pickle trays in the form of a scallop shell, and many other exquisitely produced small items. All this occurred in what is known as the "Dr. Wall" or "First Period", from 1751 to 1783.

Dr. Wall was one of the fifteen originators of the Worcester Porcelain Company. Besides being a doctor, he was also a talented artist who had painted a number of oils dealing with such historical subjects as 'Caesar being brought the head of Pompey'.

Together with a chemist named William Davis, they brought together thirteen other partners, and afterwards produced a deed which stated among other things that Dr. Wall and W. Davis "possessed the secret, art, mystery and process of making porcelain"

The so-called secret, had, in fact, come from a company in Bristol which had gone broke and had been acquired by the Worcester factory in 1752. The formula used soap rock, mined in the Lizard in Cornwall, clay from Barnstaple in Devon, and sand from the Isle of Wight.

The Worcester Porcelain Company was founded in 1751, and operated from an old mansion known as Warmstry House, situated on the left bank of the Severn, where it slowly prospered, although its very first pieces were clumsily manufactured in comparison to the factory's later work. By the early 1770's, the factory was employing 160 persons, though a very large number of them were very little boys. They worked in eleven rooms, with another set aside for the public to examine their best pieces on display, an idea that was later abandoned when it was found that the public lingered too long, and got in the way of the real business of making pottery. While it lasted, the entrance fee was putting what you pleased in a box by the gate.

In 1756, Worcester had acquired the services of Robert Hancock, an engraver who had

Left: A modern Worcester piece of Napoleon issued in a limited edition in 1969. (Collector's Guide).

Right: Another late Worcester piece by James Hadley, depicting Paul Kruger and Joseph Chamberlain. (King & Chasemore).

Below: In contrast, a pair of very rare Worcester figures of a Turk and his companion, circa 1770. (Bonhams).

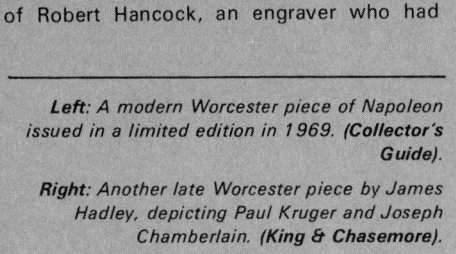

Right: A yellow round junket dish, circa 1758, and a yellow ground coffee pot with lid of the same period. Below these, a rare butter cooler, circa 1757, and a tea cup and saucer, circa 1770.

Below: An important pair of large vases in bright colours, with alternate panels of fabulous beasts. The dish is from a Duke of Gloucester service, circa 1770. Photographs courtesy of *Phillips.*

WORCESTER

worked at the Battersea enamel works and for the Bow porcelain works. Hancock introduced overglaze printing into the factory, which used on a large variety of subjects. Jugs, mugs, and punch bowls bear his work, which consisted of scenes or engraved portraits of notables of the day. Other engravers came to work for the company, but the company seems to have esteemed Hancock above the others as he eventually became a partner in the firm.

An even more positive asset to the company was the arrival of a number of Chelsea painters who had been forced to seek other employment after the illness and subsequent retirement of Nicholas Sprimont, who, as the manager of the Chelsea company, had contributed greatly to the success of the company in its early days. The Chelsea painters had been greatly influenced by Sprimont's liking for the florid and the rococo, so it was therefore inevitable that with their arrival on the scene larger and more elaborate pieces, decorated with paintings of flowers, birds or chinoiseries, surrounded by gilt scrollwork, began to appear. It is from this period also that we get some of the rich enamel ground colours that had been invented at Chelsea, including the famous Chelsea claret colour.

After the death of Dr. Wall in 1776, William Davis continued to run the factory until his own death in 1783, which led to the works being bought by Thomas Flight, whose liking for the pretentious led to some degree to the production of the dinner services previously mentioned. It marked a general decline in standards, which was not improved by a series of mergers, which saw the factory cheapening its wares and introducing a large number of transfer prints in the style of China Nakin ware.

The situation improved, however, in time, and today the Worcester Royal Porcelain Company Ltd., can look back on more than two hundred years of uninterrupted production, in which, for all its ups and downs, it has still managed to make itself one of the major names in the history of English porcelain.

It should be noted finally, that an enormous number of fakes and reproductions were produced in the late 19th century. Many of the reproductions were made by the firm of Samson in Paris, who, since 1845, specialised in making copies of early porcelain. Many of them bear an S mark.

BOOKS

Worcester Porcelain by Stanley Fisher.
Old English Porcelain by W.B. Honey.
The Illustrated Guide to Worcester Porcelain by Henry Sandon.
Coloured Worcester Porcelain by H. Rissik Marshall.

MUSEUMS

Worcester: Dyson Perrins Museum
London: The British Museum and the Victoria and Albert Museum.
Bristol: City Museum.
Dealers: Most major dealers carry at least one or two pieces of Worcester.

*Right – from top to bottom: A pair of ewers of classical shape. Red cardinals, from a series of Birds of America. A pair of vases, circa 1911. Photographs Courtesy of **The Collector's Guide**.*

STAND & DELIVER

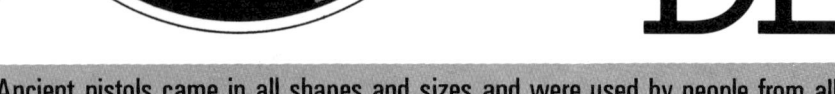

Ancient pistols came in all shapes and sizes and were used by people from all walks of life, ranging from highwaymen to ladies who carried them in their muffs as a weapon of defence. But most of them had one thing in common. They were beautifully made — which has made them highly prized.

In the 18th century, most towns and cities in Britain were infested with footpads and highwaymen, who held up stage coaches with monotonous regularity. Highwaymen rode openly into Hyde Park at dusk, where they tied their horses to the railings before sallying forth to rob sedan chairs, carriages and pedestrians indiscriminately. In Kensington Gardens, a bell was rung nightly to warn people to gather together in large parties for their own protection. In this climate, it was hardly surprising that guns were made which were essentially defence weapons. These ranged from tiny muff pistols to single shot flintlocks, which could be carried in the waistband or pocket. Double barrelled pistols fitted with a retractable bayonet were also available.

Another form of self defence was the blunderbuss, often carried by coachmen or used for the defence of one's property. Contrary to popular belief, they did not fire rusty nails, but were loaded with some 20 to 40 small lead balls.

But pistols were not produced merely for self defence. With duelling so much a part of the gentlemen or officer's life, a ready made market existed which the gun makers were not slow to exploit.

Pistols made especially for duelling began to appear at the end of the 18th century. They were sold as pairs, complete with accessories, and fitted in a case of oak or mahogany. These dueling sets are greatly prized by collectors, particularly those made by Joseph Manton, who was regarded in his day as one of the finest gunsmiths in the country. The pistols of H.W. Mortimer, of Fleet Street, London, who specialised in flintlocks, and the superbly finished pistols of John Twigg of Piccadilly, London, are also greatly sought after, as are some of the highly ornate French and Belgian pistols, with chiselling and carving on their barrels and stocks.

As the life and death of a duellist depended on a single shot, a great deal of time was spent in trying to make a duelling pistol as accurate as possible. But they still remained inaccurate, until a way was found to rifle the barrel, which spun the bullet, so that when it left the muzzle, the bullet was still spinning, which helped to

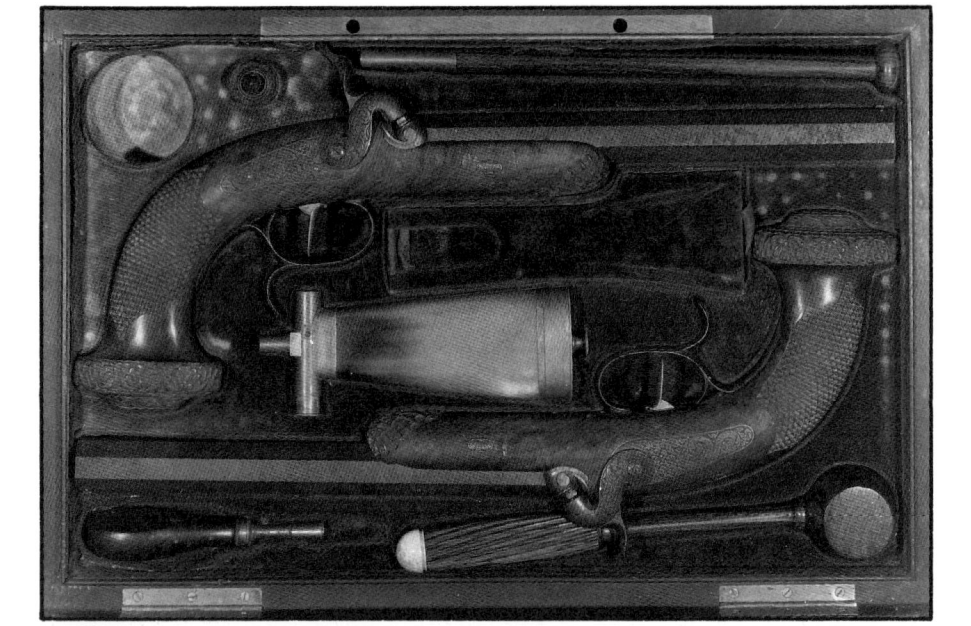

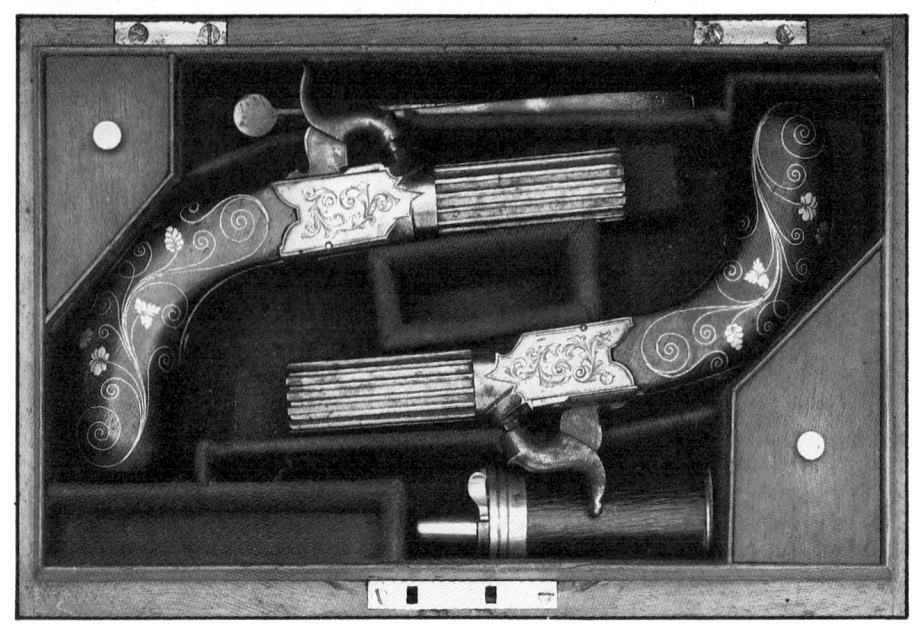

Top left*. A pair of percussion rifled target pistols. Circa 1850.*

Left*. A pair of percussion box Lock pocket pistols.*
PHILLIPS

cancel out some of the pistol's basic faults.

But as rifling was considered by a large number of duellists to be unsporting, many of the pistols were then made heavier to reduce the recoil, and a charge designed to send the ball spinning in a flat trajectory which kept it on course.

The accuracy of hand weapons was greatly increased, however, with the introduction of the revolver, a single barrelled pistol with a revolving breech, containing a number of chambers for the cartridges, which allowed its user to fire off several shots without having to reload.

The first revolver was the pepper box, which was fired with a percussion cap, with the whole barrel revolving in one piece when it was fired. The first use of a form of pepper pot dates back as far as the 17th century, but the weapon was cumbersome, difficult to fire, and wildly inaccurate. The ones produced in England in the middle of the 19th century were an improvement, but still left much to be desired.

It was left to an American, Samuel Colt to patent in 1836 the first really efficient revolving pistol, which was later adopted by the US Army.

By 1848, after many of his revolvers had been sold for use in the Mexican War of 1846-8, Colt decided to extend his business activities to London, where he built a factory at Pimlico in 1853. His venture was so succesful that the factory produced and sold some 50,000 revolvers in the four years of its existence.

Another major American company producing revolvers came into being in 1854, when Horace Smith went into partnership with Daniel B. Wesson. In their workshops in Springfield, Massachussetts, they began to make a revolver for a metallic rim cartridge, for which they had an exclusive monopoly until 1869, when their patent expired. Colt was then able to re-adapt their guns to take in the Smith and Wesson design, while also bringing out a new pocket weapon which became very popular and was still being used at the beginning of the 20th century.

Colt did not live to see his factory invent what is perhaps the most famous of all revolvers — The Peacemaker. Never was there a more inaccurate description.

Although it was popular with lawmen in the West, it was also used by professional gunmen and trigger happy men who saw the Peacemaker as the ultimate 'equaliser'.

"God did not make all men equal," Westerners were fond of saying. "But Colt's revolver did."

1. A flintlock rifle. The gun was used at the battle of Wexford Bridge 1798.

2. An early 18th century silver mounted pistol.

3. A coaching blunderbuss.

4. A silver mounted Flintlock Boxlock cannon barrelled pistol. Circa 1750.

5. An early duelling pistol.

PHILLIPS

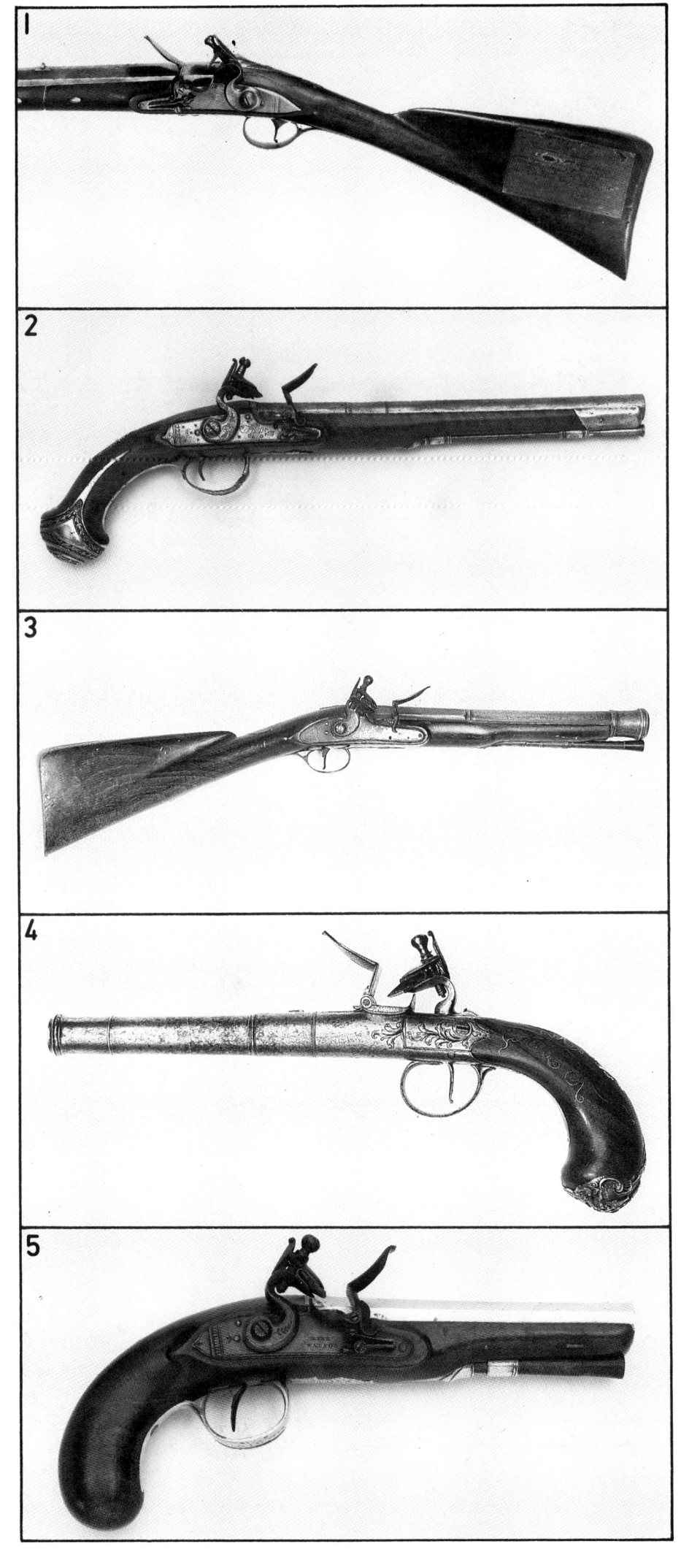

Certainly with a Colt in his hand, even a weakling stood a fair chance in a gun fight — providing he knew how to use it. Even so, the Peacemaker was not the perfect weapon, as its short barrel reduced its power and accuracy to a relatively short distance.

A short article such as this could not hope to encompass the history of the pistol, which dates back to the 17th century, when it was invented in Pistoria, Italy, by Caminello Vitelli, who flourished around 1650. Fortunately, a large number of books have been written on the subject, and some of them, at least, should be consulted by anyone who is thinking of building up his own collection of pistols. But before

doing so, bear in mind that under the Firearms Act of 1937, guns that are kept as collector's pieces must be at least 100 years old before they are excluded from the need to have a firearms certificate. This confines the collector mainly to percussion pieces and flintlocks.

As we have said elsewhere in this book, when buying, go either to the auction rooms or to a reliable dealer. If you *must* go looking for bargains on the stalls (and they can sometimes be found) at least make sure you know something about the subject first, otherwise you're likely to land up with a fake on your hands.

How common are fakes, anyway? The simple answer to that, is more than there should be.

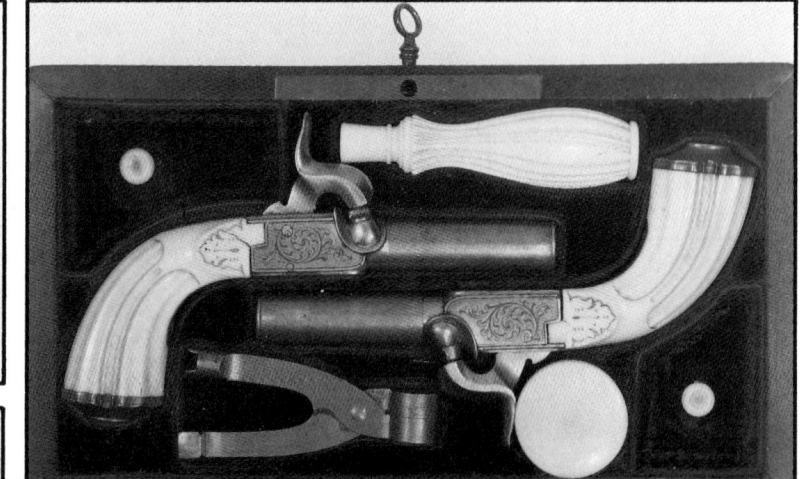

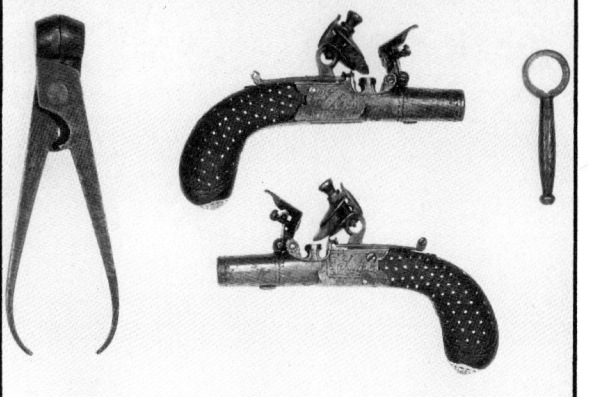

Top above. *A rare flintlock four barrelled Ducks Foot pistol.*

Above. *A pair of miniature flintlock pistols. Circa 1810. These are genuine working miniatures, complete with barrel key and bullet mould.*

Top right. *A cased pair of percussion pocket pistols. Made in Paris for a Swedish nobleman.*

Right. *A scarce five-shot 80 bore percussion revolver. Signed Westley Richards, 170 New Bond St., London.*

REFERENCE BOOKS

Duelling Pistols	J.A. Atkinson	The Book of the Gun	H.L. Peterson
Encyclopedia of		Old Guns and Pistols	N. Boston
Firearms	H.L. Peterson	The Revolver 1865-1888	
	and Robin May		A.W.E. Taylerson
Small Arms	F. Wilkinson		
Antique Firearms	F. Wilkinson	American Books	
European and American Arms	C. Blair	The Treasury of the Gun	H.L. Peterson
English, Irish and Scottish Firearms Makers		The Revolver 1818-1865	L.P. Peterson
	A. Carey	Pepperbox Firearms	L. Winant.

MUSEUMS

London — Tower of London Armouries
Victoria and Albert Museum
Glasgow — Art Gallery and Museum

the glory of GLASS

According to Pliny, the Roman historian, glass was discovered by accident by some Phoenician traders who had stopped to cook themselves a meal on the sandy banks of the River Belus, under Mount Carmel. After using some blocks of natron (an impure form of carbonate of soda), as a base for their pots, they found that the heat from the fire had fused the sand and soda to form a glass-like substance. Although one cannot completely discard this as being a myth, the Syrian glass makers later actually used sand from the banks of this particular river.

Although the ancient Egyptians had a glass making industry, the making of glass on a major scale did not occur until the days of Imperial Rome, when it was used for an amazing number of purposes. As well as producing goblets, jars, bottles, coloured table ware and many other pieces of domestic ware, the Romans introduced the idea of using thin plates of glass as a coating for their walls, and also invented a glass cutting technique which was not equalled until the 17th century, when the Germans invented a new technique of their own for cutting glass. This can be seen at its best in the work of a master engraver like Gottfried Spiller (see large picture over).

It had been introduced into Germany from Bohemia (now Czechoslovakia) where the Bohemians had been cutting glass before the 17th century, using engravers who were particularly skilful at engraving landscapes. They dominated the scene until the 1840's, when the French became a major force in the same period with their millefiori paperweights. *See article Miracles in Glass.*

By this time, the once famous Venetian glass industry had gone into decline. It had been producing glass since 1450, on the Island of Murano, where the glass workers had been so strictly controlled for a while, that

A goblet by William Beilby (1740-1819), who worked with his sister, Mary, first in Newcastle, then in Fife, Scotland.

GLASS

they faced a heavy punishment if they attempted to leave the island. Among their many contributions the Venetians had brought to the art of glass making was the means of making crackle glass, a process in which a half blown object is suddenly cooled and then re-heated and expanded until the surface becomes crazed. But neither this nor any of their other innovations could stand up to the competition from other countries. The popular demand for cut glass added to its eventual collapse, as the thinness of Venetian glass made it unsuitable for cutting. By the time of the Great Exhibition of 1851, Venice no longer even had a glass guild, and was unable to send a single object for exhibition.

But the industry did revive to some degree soon afterwards, when the Compania Venezia-Murano was founded by Antonio Salviati, who began producing a large number of pieces in the old Murano manner.

English glass did not really establish itself until 1676, when George Ravenscroft was encouraged by the Glass Seller's Company to produce a glass of lead, or flint glass, that was less likely to shatter than Venetian glass. Ravenscroft set up a glass factory at Henley-on-Thames, but unfortunately his early efforts developed 'glass sickness', a crizzling in which fine cracks appeared in the glass. After this fault was ironed out by the use of lead oxide, Ravenscroft went on to become the most famous of all English glass makers.

In 1745, the English glass makers suddenly found themselves greatly handicapped by the Glass Excise Act, in which a duty was levied of 'one penny per pound' weight for all the ingredients that went into the making of glass'. This was to cripple the English glass industry for nearly a century, before the Act was repealed in 1845. The repeal created a rebirth of the glass making industry, particularly in the Stourbridge factories in and around Worcester, where an entire school of cameo cutters and engravers came into being.

Irish glass was exempted from the Act, which the Irish glass makers were not slow to exploit. In 1783, the Waterford Glass Company was established by George and William Penrose, whose factory soon became particularly well known for its use of glass cutting as a means of ornamentation — a reputation which it has maintained to the present day.

A large number of books have been published on glass. You will find the following useful:

An Illustrated Dictionary of Glass by Harold Newman.
A History of English and Irish Glass by W.A. Thorpe.
The Collector's Dictionary of Glass by E.M. Elville.
Glass Through the Ages by E. Barrington Haynes.
Old Glass by O.N. Wilkinson.

If you're interested in buying antique glass, try:

Arenski, 29-31 George Street, London W1.
S.W. Parry (Old Glass), 16 Paddington Green, London W2.
Sommervale Antiques, 6 Radstock Road, Midsomer Norton, Avon. (By appointment).

Above. *A Mary Gregory glass enamelled dish.* **Below.** *A standing bowl and cover, with flat geometric cutting.* **Right.** *Top to bottom. Scent bottle containing a crystallo ceramic portrait of Princess Charlotte. A Bohemian enamelled flask. A Scottish presentation goblet, dated 1824.* **Far right.** *Jar and cover, probably engraved by Gottfried Spiller, circa 1700.* Photographs: courtesy of **Antique Dealer** and **Collectors Guide.**

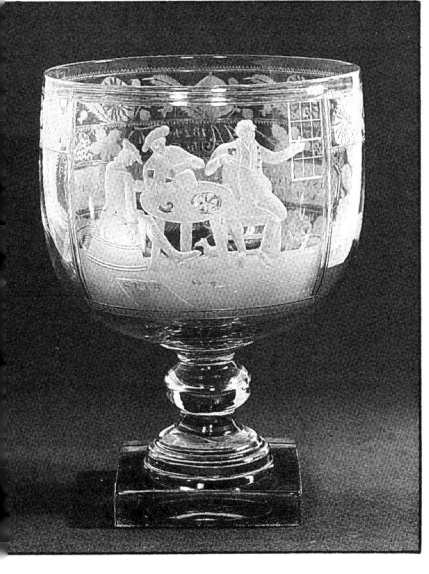

Thanks perhaps to TV programmes like 'The Antiques Road Show', there has been a tremendous upsurge of interest in antiques, which has also made it possible for those who have watched the programmes to acquire at least a little knowledge on the subject. People, too, have come to realise that, generally speaking, antiques as an investment are a good thing.

But in Central London, in particular, people who want to buy antiques hesitate to browse around antique shops. The prices can be formidable and the manner of their owners often off-putting. Not unnaturally, therefore, the newcomer to the field of antiques tends to head for the nearest antique centre, where he can wander around unmolested. If he should happen to pause at a stall, he will generally receive a friendly welcome. Quite often the stalls are run by amateurs themselves, who have acquired enough knowledge to set themselves up in business, and this does tend to lead to a better

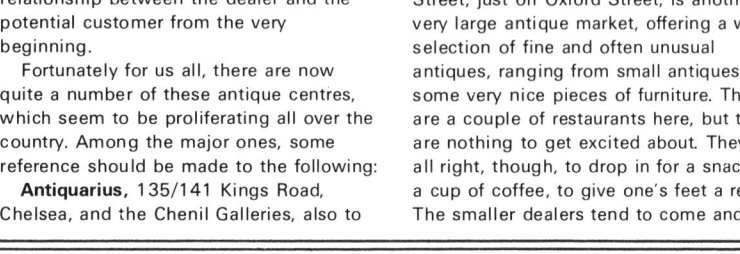

Horse on wheels. Circa 1833, and a French barking dog. Circa 1895. **Antiquarius.**

relationship between the dealer and the potential customer from the very beginning.

Fortunately for us all, there are now quite a number of these antique centres, which seem to be proliferating all over the country. Among the major ones, some reference should be made to the following:

Antiquarius, 135/141 Kings Road, Chelsea, and the Chenil Galleries, also to be found in the Kings Road, both with opening hours from 10am to 6pm, Monday to Saturday.

Both Antiquarius and the Chenil Galleries have a large range of quality antiques, as good as any you will find in any antique centre. As they both are almost on top of each other, you could spend a full morning going around both of them to some advantage. When you leave, exhausted , there are dozens of restaurants

A selection of silver, glass and enamel inkwells. 1880-1920 **Antiquarius.**

to chose from in this trendy area.

Although the **Bond Street Centre** at 124 Bond Street, W1, is situated in an expensive area for antiques, we found most of the items here very reasonably priced. It is a much smaller centre than the others we've just mentioned and certainly much quieter — probably because people think the antiques on sale here are going to be expensive, as it is in Bond Street. Which is rather a shame, as there are some very good quality antiques to be found here. Open 10am to 5.45pm. Saturday to 4pm.

Grays Antique Centre, at 58 Davies Street, just off Oxford Street, is another very large antique market, offering a wide selection of fine and often unusual antiques, ranging from small antiques to some very nice pieces of furniture. There are a couple of restaurants here, but they are nothing to get excited about. They are all right, though, to drop in for a snack or a cup of coffee, to give one's feet a rest. The smaller dealers tend to come and go, not because the overheads here are heavy, which they are not, considering the area, but, one suspects, because they have not been selling the right items. Grays, by the way, claim to have the best selection of antique jewellery in the world. Wandering around the centre, one can well believe their claim.

In addition to the main building, there is another section of Grays at 1-7 Davies Mews, just at the rear of the centre, which is almost as large as the main building.

Grays Antique markets, have a whole floor of repair workshops, a Bureau de Change, and furthermore undertakes that in the event of a bonafide private buyer purchasing from one of their stalls an item up to £1,000 which is not in accordance with the description on the official bill of sale, to refund the money. You really cannot ask for more.

Two other important antique centres are **Alfies Antique Market,** 13 to 25 Church Street, Marylebone, London NW8, and the **Camden Passage Centre,** 357 Upper Street, London N1.

Alfies is a veritable rabbit warren of antique dealers' stalls and showrooms housed in what was once a Victorian department store. Which will give you some idea of its size. It has some 200 dealers there, all clamouring for your attention — in the nicest possible way. You can buy practically anything here, even old gramophone records and horn gramophones. Certainly, it's a real Aladin's Cave, stuffed with goodies, mixed up with other somewhat less desirable items.

Austro Hungarian silver gilt ink stand 1800. **Antiquarius.**

CONTINUED OVERLEAF

Amersham, Buckinghamshire

The Old part of Amersham is worth a visit in itself. The Olde Town is full of interesting buildings and a number of antique shops. Also to be found there is the **Old Amersham Antiques Centre,** which can be found at 20-22 Whielden Street. Open Monday to Saturday, 9am to 6pm.

Ampthill, Bedfordshire

The Ampthill Antique Centre in the Market Square, is spread over four floors, and worth a visit if you are in the area. It generally has a wide range of antiques, and is open Tuesday to Sunday, 10am to 5.30pm.

Bath, Avon

The Bartlett Street Centre at 9 Bartlett Street, is on two floors and offers the usual range of general antiques. The last time were there, it had a nice cafe. Open Monday to Saturday, 9.30am to 5pm.

Great Western Antiques Centre also in Bartlett Street. This is a very large centre and carries a large range of items. A must if you are in Bath. Open Monday to Saturday, 9.30am to 5pm. Wednesday from 8am to 4.30pm.

Battlebridge, Essex

The **Battlebridge Antique Centre,** housed in the Old Granary at Wickford, is another large and interesting centre worth visiting. It's located off the A130 by-pass between Wickford and Chelmsford. Open daily.

Birmingham, West Midlands

The Birmingham Antique Centre, at 141 Bromsgrove Street, has been there for a long time — since 1966, to be precise. Worth a visit, but open only on Thursdays, from 9am.

Boscombe, Bournemouth, Dorset

The Antiques Centre here is to be found at 837/839 Christchurch Road. It has the advantage of being fairly close to quite a number of antique shops, which, all in all, will keep you occupied for the best part of a day. Open Monday to Saturday 9.30am to 5.30pm.

Bristol, Avon

The Clifton Antiques Market is to be found in The Mall, fairly close to Brunel's suspension bridge. The area is worth walking around, anyway, as there are a number of nice Georgian houses to be seen and some good restaurants in the area. Open Tuesday to Saturday 10am to 6pm.

Canterbury, Kent

Canterbury Antiques and Craft Market is a fairly small centre, but as it's on the tourist track, it's worth mentioning. It's in St Peters Street, and open only on Saturday, 9.30am to 5pm.

Chester, Cheshire

Chester Antiques Centre, which is to be found at 41 Lower Bridge Street, is another small centre, but all the dealers offer quality goods. It is, moreover, housed in a pleasant Georgian house within an historic area. Open Monday to Saturday 10am to 5pm.

Coggeshall, Essex

Coggeshall Antique Centre at Doubleday Corner, deals with a large range of antiques, and has the added advantage of having quite a number of antique shops in the vicinity. Open Monday to Saturday 10am to 5pm.

Coltishall, Norfolk

Eric Bates & Sons, lying north of Norwich, is very definitely worth a visit, as they offer one of the largest selections available in the North East. You can get almost everything here from furniture to small antiques. A packing service is also available. It is in the High Street, and is open from 9am to 5pm, Mondays to Fridays, 10am to 5pm on Saturdays.

While you are visiting the above, you can also look around **Coltishall Antiques Centre,** also in the High Street. Hours 10am to 5pm, Monday to Saturday.

East Molesey, Surrey

The Antique and Craft Arcade at 77 Bridge Street is worth a look if you are in the area, especially as it is close to **The Hampton Court Revival,** also in Bridge Street. Both of these are located in the antiques area around Hampton Court, which means you can combine looking around Hampton Court with a good browse around the antique shops.

The former of these two centres is open from 10am to 5pm, Monday to Saturday. The same applies to the **Hampton Court Revival,** which closes on Wednesday.

Gloucester

The Gloucester Antiques Centre, which has been going since 1979, is centred in Severn Road, and housed in a large warehouse. This is a large centre, covering some 30,000 square feet, and therefore well worth a visit. Its hours are varied, though. Monday to Friday 9.30am to 5pm; Saturday, 9.30am to 4.30pm There are generally a lot of dealers here — so have a good day. One should add that there's an extra bonus with this centre. It's also open on Sundays 1pm to 5pm.

Harrogate, North Yorkshire

West Park Antiques Pavillion at 20 West Park has the advantage of being near some 200 acres of Parkland, and very near a large number of antique shops. Anyway, Harrogate is a very nice place to stay overnight. Open Tuesday to Saturdays, 10am to 5pm.

Hitchen, Hertfordshire

The Hitchen Antiques Gallery at 37 Bridge Street is a small centre, but worth visiting if only because it occupies a charming beamed Tudor building. (It was built in 1580). Open Monday to Saturday 10am to 5.30pm.

Hungerford, Berkshire

Hungerford Arcade, 26 High Street has a large number of dealers there, offering a wide range of antiques. Open Monday to Saturday, 9.30am to 5.30pm.

Hythe, Kent

Malthouse Arcade is in the High Street, offers a fairly large range of small antiques. Hythe is a charming little town in which you can also amuse yourself examining the 2,000 human skulls and 8,000 thigh bones to be found in the crypt of St Leonard's Church — if that's the sort of thing you like doing. The Malthouse Arcade is open only on Friday and Saturday and on the Monday Bank Holiday. 10am to 6pm.

Leek, Staffordshire

Aspleys Antique Imports and Exports. We have included this one because it is situated in a good area for buying antiques. It is worth a visit, anyway, if you're in Leek, or nearby. Open Monday to Saturday, 9am to 6pm.

Lewes, Sussex

Lewes Antique Centre, 20 Cliffe High Street, has been going since 1974, but by and large we found the stock, with the exception of a few items, nothing to get excited about. Most of it is for the lower end of the market, and therefore not likely to be of much interest for rich American tourists. But, as with all antique markets, you *could* be lucky.

Lincoln

Eastgate Antique Centre. Situated near the Cathedral, this centre is at Black Horse Chambers, 6 Eastgate, and was originally part of an old coaching inn. It's on the small side, but there are generally quite a number of good items to be found. If you're going there don't approach it from the town by way of The Steep, unless you're very fit. Even cars cannot make it up this walk, so you have been warned. Coming down is fine, especially as there are a number of antique shops to be seen on the way.

CONTINUED OVERLEAF

LONDON

ANTIQUE·CENTRES

A collection of antique inkwells. **Antiquarius.**

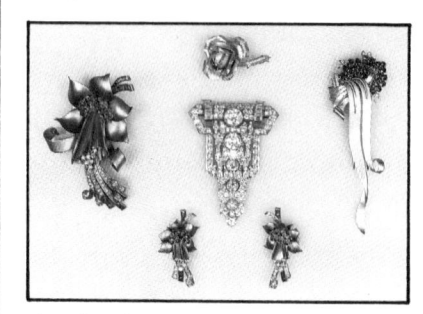

Jewellery from **The Bond Antique Centre.**

A Tang Chinese camel. **Grays.**

Edison Gem phonograph. Circa 1905. **Grays.**

Alfies claim that as their dealers turnover their stuff so fast, prices tend to be cheaper there than anywhere else. Alfiesis open Tuesday to Saturday, 10am to 6pm.

The Camden Passage Antiques Centre, consists of five arcades and five market areas within 200 yards, with 350 dealers offering enough antiques to send you away, quite bemused with it all. If all this was not enough to contend with, there is the **Camden Antique Market,** where some sixty dealers sell stamps, prints, Beatles memorabilia, and a host of other small items. **Plus** all this are all the antique shops which have helped to take over this area. Be prepared, therefore, to make a day of it, pausing only to have a pleasant lunch at one of the several very good restaurants there. But be careful with your timing. The Camden Passage Antiques Centre is only open Wednesday and Saturday; Books, Thursday.

The Camden Antique market is open from 7am, Thursday.

Other antique markets and centres include: The **Antique Exchange,** Bermondsey Square, London SE1. This opens on Thursday only, 12 noon to 6pm. Offers a large selection of bric-a-brac and various other small items. Near Tower Bridge.

Bermondsey Market, at the corner of Long Lane and Bermondsey Street. This consists of several warehouses, containing some 130 dealers. This is an internationally important trade market, selling some very interesting pieces. Don't let the word 'trade' put you off. Anybody's money is welcome, as long as they are prepared to get there at five in the morning, which is when the trading begins. It ends at 2pm, but by then all the good stuff has long since gone. The nearest tube station is either Tower Hill, or Borough. We think this is really worth visiting, as you're really among the professionals here.

Cutler Street Antique Market, Goulston Street, EC1. Open Sunday morning from 7am. This is by the famous Petticoat Lane Market, also open Sunday mornings, so you could make quite a morning of it. One should add that this is really a specialist market for those interested in gold, silver, jewellery, gems, coins and stamps.

Dixons Antique Market, 471 Upper Richmond Road West, East Sheen, SW14. Open Thursday to Tuesday, 10am to 5.30pm. There's some 30 dealers here, offering quite a nice range of goods, including Art Nouveau glass, and Art pieces.

Hampstead Antique Emporium, 12 Heath Street, London NW3. This is a pleasant place to visit as its in the heart of Hampstead village. The market, which has been there since 1967, is open Tuesday to Saturday, 10am to 6pm, has 24 dealers there, selling small antiques. Take the tube to Hampstead if you are not going there by car.

'Palais Royale' monocular and needlecase, a miniature telescope and gentlemen's necessaire. **Grays.**

1920 'Asprey' Fantasy Mascot. **Grays.**

Grey pearls, diamond and platinum clasp, 1930s. **Grays.**

Set of four Flemish ivory Seasons on ebonied bases. Circa 1800. **Grays.**

Manchester
Royal Exchange Antiques Gallery. This is has a good range of collector's items, and is open Monday to Saturday, 10am to 5pm. While in the city, also call in at Antiques Hypermarket, Old Town Hall, 965 Stockport Road.

Marlborough, Wiltshire
London House Antique Centre, in the High Street, offers a wide range of general antiques, as well as pottery and porcelain from the 18/19th century. Open Monday to Saturday, 9.30am to 5.30pm.

Needham Market, Suffolk
Needham Market Antique Centre, which can be found at the Town Hall, in the High Street, is spread out on two floors. As well as offering the usual range of antiques, it has a jewellery and clocks workshop. Open Monday to Saturday 10am to 5pm.

Newark, Nottinghamshire
Castle Gate Antique Centre. This is a fairly recent addition to the centres springing up all over England. Situated at 55 Castle Gate in a listed Georgian building, its three floors contain a lot of collectable items. Open Monday to Saturday, 9am to 5pm.

Newton Abbot, Devon
Newton Abbot Antiques Centre. This has been going since 1973, and is situated in 55 East Street, which is easy to find as it is in the town centre. It has more than 50 stands selling anything from furniture to books, but is only open on Tuesdays between 9am and 4pm.

Norwich, Norfolk
As Norwich does not have as many antique shops as one might expect in a city of this nature, one's immediate inclination is to visit an antique centre. The one here is the **Norwich Antique and Collectors Centre,** which proved something of a disappointment. But to be fair, we did visit it at the worst time of the year (January) which may have accounted for its indifferent stock and general air of apathy. It has been going since 1982, so it must have something at other times of the year. It's situated at Quayside, a pleasant location by the river. Open Monday to Saturday, 10am to 5.30pm, including Bank Holidays.

Nottingham
Top Hat Antiques Centre, 72 Derby Road. The dealers there carry a wide variety of antiques. Open Monday to Saturday, 9.30am to 5pm.

Petersfield, Hampshire
The House of Antiques at 4 College Street, was established in 1979, and offers a wide range of antiques. Open Monday to Saturday, 9.30am to 5pm (1pm Thursdays).

Colin Macleod's Antique Centre is a must for anyone anywhere near the area. The Antique Centre can be found at 159/161 Goldsmith's Avenue, also has nine adjacent warehouses, filled with a large range of antiques, with the emphasis on furniture. In addition, it offers a number fo services, such as stripping and polishing furniture, upholstery, plus a packing and shipping service.

St Albans, Hertfordshire
St Albans Antique Market at the Town Hall, is only open Mondays, 9.30am to 4pm. But quite a few dealers are there and the stock is always changing.

Sandwich, Kent
Noah's Ark Antique Market at 5 King Street, has been going for some years and it is situated in a 16th century house. Open Monday to Saturday, with the exception of Wednesday, 10am to 5pm. Its dealers carry good stocks in most areas, which is perhaps hardly surprising when one thinks of the visitors who go to Sandwich, which is an unspoilt medieval town of much interest to most visitors.

Sawbridgeworth, Hertfordshire
Herts and Essex Antique Centre. To be found at the Maltings, Station Road, where some hundred dealers occupy its three floors. An attractive centre with a Bistro and coffee shop. It has the additional merit of being right by the railway station — a useful bonus for those who should decided to travel there by rail. If you're going by car, there are good parking facilities at the centre.

Shrewsbury, Shropshire
Shrewsbury Antique Centre is worth visiting as it is used by the trade quite a lot for obtaining new stock. A sufficient recommendation in itself. It is to be found in Princess Street and is open several days a week, 9.30am to 5.30pm. Use it as an excuse for visiting Shrewsbury, if you haven't been there before. It is full of wonderful black and white buildings, and has been visited by no end of famous people, including Charles Dickens, the singer Jenny Lind, and the violinist, Paganini.

The Antique Centre has some 40 dealers offering a really large range of antiques.

Stone, Staffordshire
Stone Antique Centre, at Bridge House, 56 Newcastle Road. It is closed on Mondays, but is open for the rest of the week from Tuesday to Saturday, 10.30am to 5pm. It has been going since 1981, and the dealers there sell everything from furniture to small collector's items.

Stratford-upon-Avon, Warwickshire
The Antique Arcade. This is situated in Sheep Street, and although small is worth visiting if you are in Stratford. Open Monday 10.30am to 5.30pm.

Stratford Antique Centre, Ely Street. This is quite a large centre with 50 dealers selling all manner of antiques. Open 10am to 6pm.

Needless to say with a busy tourist town of this nature which attracts tourists from all over the world, there are dozesn of antique shops to look at as well as the markets.

Tewkesbury, Gloucester
Tewkesbury is another old town which is steeped in history. It was the site of the Yorkist victory in the War of the Roses. Besides being full of old hostelries, including the Royal Hop Pole Inn, built in the 14th century and mentioned in *The Pickwick Papers,* it has the **Tewkesbury Antique Centre,** which has extensive showrooms, with its dealers offering the sort of quality antiques you will find in all the better antique markets. It is at 78 Church Street, very close to the Abbey, and is open Monday to Saturday, 9.30am to 5pm.

Twyford, Buckinghamshire
Twyford Antique Centre, 1 High Street. This pretty little village is noted for its associations with two people — Benjamin Franklin who wrote some of his autobiography there, and Alexander Pope, who was expelled from its local school.

The Antique Centre here opens Tuesday to Saturday, 9.30am to 5.30pm. Reasonable amount of quality stock which seems to turn over quickly.

Wallingford, Oxfordshire
Although you've probably never heard of Wallingford, it was once an important town and a Royalist stronghold in the Civil War, until it was finally forced to surrender to the Parliamentary army. Today, it is a pleasant market town and riverside resort. For the antique collector who is not interested in history, there is **The Lamb's Antique Centre** in the High St. 10 am. to 5 pm., but closed on Wednesday and Sunday.

ART DECO

STYLISED ELEGANCE

Although the style of Art Deco began immediately after World War I, it owes its name to *L'Exposition Internationale des Arts Decoratifs et Industriels Moderne,* held in Paris in 1925.

It was not, strictly speaking, an international exhibition, as it had been underwritten by the French Government, mainly to promote the work being done by its own artists and craftsmen. In that respect the exhibition was a highly successful one, as it established the French as arbiters of current taste.

Art Deco as an art form was something that belonged very much to the twenties, even though it lasted until 1939, when its reign ended with the advent of World War II. Its whole feeling is redolent of the age when it was born, the age of the 'flapper' and fast cars, of afternoon *thé dansants,* jazz bands and night clubs. It covered everything from the decor used in Diaghilev's Ballet Russe to the glass of Rene Lalique. And nowhere was it more perfectly expressed than in the figurines of Lorenzl, D.H. Chiparus and F.D. Preis. Producing figurines of this nature even engaged the attention of a serious sculptor like Jacob Epstein, who was one of the few whose work was produced only in limited editions, unlike his fellow artists, whose figurines were made in large quantities. To begin with they were made in ivory, porcelain and bronze, but as their popularity grew, the manufacturers began making cheap versions in spelter (zinc) and simulated ivory made from plastic. These figurines, which were mostly of nudes or highly stylized dancers standing on an onyx base, were later copied in enormous quantities, and are practically worthless. So don't be tempted if you see a figure standing in the window of a junk shop. The originals fetch very fancy prices and won't be found in such places.

The Art Deco form pervaded everything, from the fitting and design of a cinema to

---

It was the age of the 'flapper', of **thé dansants,** fast cars, jazz and night clubs, and its spirit was epitomised by a new art form that was born in the Paris of the twenties . . .

---

small pieces of pottery and metalwork. Furniture designers, although avoiding the radical outlines of furniture made by people like Mackintosh and Walter Gropius, father of the Bahaus movement, still rejected at first the elegant for the functional, though often using such exotic details as ivory handles and luxurious coverings. It was the heyday of chromium metal, cast in stark outlines, and considered today by many as an abomination, fit only for use in office furniture. Later, however, the vogue for plain furniture died out and brightly coloured lacquered furniture which blended modern design with traditional styles began to appear.

As was inevitable with something that had become a highly popular art form, a great deal of *kitsch* rubbish was produced, including hideous looking bakelite wireless sets and household ware, covered with geometric designs, which can be seen gathering dust on many a junk stall today.

Nevertheless, high standards were still being maintained in other areas. Despite the mounds of rubbish on sale, good pieces of silver and table ware could be found at Liberty's, who employed their own designers who were generally members of a Guild. Surprisingly, Art Deco does not seem to have had any significant influence on pottery, with the notable exception of a few English potters such as Clarice Cliff, possible because painted pottery and porcelain had suddenly become less fashionable around that time.

Probably the most famous of all the names in the Art Deco field is that of Rene Lalique, who had already made an enormous reputation for himself during the Art Nouveau period of the 1890's, with his revolutionary approach to jewellery design, in which he had broken all the canons of jewellery making by abandoning the fashion for large stones in favour of small semi-precious stones in highly original settings.

But although Lalique was considered to be

Left. *Lalique:* **Victoire.** *A frosted and polished glass car mascot, commonly referred to as 'Spirit of the Wind'.*

Below. *A Tambourine dancer, in painted bronze and ivory with onyx tambourine by Lorenzl.*

Lalique: **Cinq Cheveaux** *five prancing horses in silhouette.*

the greatest of all the modern jewellers, his interest in it began to fade, which fortuitously coincided with the waving of the public's interest in Art Nouveau.

Lalique had already done a little experimenting with glass. Now he decided the time had come for him to devote his full attention to glass making. In 1902, he established a small workshiop in Clairefontaine, near Ramboillet, where he began producing statuettes and vases.

He was still only operating on a small scale, when the *perfumier,* Francois Coty, allowed him to design some of his bottles. It was his first big step into the commercial field, and he quickly became so successful that he had to open another workshop. By the time of the Paris exhibition, he had become the leading exponent of decorative glass ware, and his displays at the exhibition further enhanced his reputation.

Lalique's glass was quite unique. Whereas all the other glassmakers used vari-coloured designs, his were mostly made with lead crystal, which gave them a faintly misty look. They were also mass produced.

Although a craftsman of the first rank, Lalique's approach to his work as a glass maker was strictly commercial. His aim was still not an unworthy one — to make available to the public as many reproductions of his work as possible, at prices which most people could afford. Hundreds of copies were made of each piece, mostly with motifs from nature or of female figures. Because of their originality all his work was in great demand both in France and England.

Lalique died in 1945, leaving behind him a large output of work which ranged from large pieces to tiny ashtrays and radiator caps, of all things.

From all the foregoing, anyone might be forgiven for thinking that France dominated the Art Deco scene throughout the years of its short life. But this was far from being the case. Soon after the Paris exhibition, the United

States challenged France's supremacy with more than a little success. New York's Radio City Music Hall, whose interior and fittings were designed by Donald Deskey, is one of the more notable examples of how successfully the Americans embraced Art Deco.

Later, after an exhibition from Paris had toured the country, Macey's stores hit on the idea of staging its own exhibition called Art In Trade. More exhibitions of the same nature were staged, and eventually a debased form of Art Deco appeared, which became known as Moderne. In an attempt to counteract this movement, the Metropolitan Museum eventually held an exhibition, but too much emphasis was laid on objects which had been mass produced for it to change things. Not that it mattered very much any more. For by then Art Deco was already beginning to seem dated.

If you are interested in reading more on this subject, a number of well written and lavishly illustrated books are available:

Right. A figurine of a Fan Dancer in bronze and ivory with green onyx tray base.

Below right. Figurine of a snake dancer in painted bronze and ivory, with onyx base, by Chiparus.

Below. Figurine of an Andalusian Dancer in bronze and ivory, with bronze and black marble base.

Art Deco by Victor Arwas.
Lalique by Victor Arwas.
Glass: Art Nouveau to Art Deco by Victor Arwas.
Art Deco Poster Graphics by Jean Delhaye.
(All PUB Academy Editions)
Lalique for Collectors by Katharine Morrison McClinton.

All photographs by courtesy of Editions Graphics, Clifford Street, London W1.

COLLECTING CLOCKS

The steps taken from measuring time by the hourglass or sun dial to making a mechanical clock that counted off the hours and the minutes is something we know little about beyond that it took part in the 14th century, which is when we have our first written reports of mechanical clocks. These refer to the tower clock that Roger Stoke made for Norwich Cathedral, and the one made by Richard of Wallingford, the abbot of St. Albans, who claimed that it took him thirty years to make.

Although we know that a number of tower clocks were made by blacksmiths in the last part of the 15th century, knowledge of what the horologists were up to remains minimal until the 16th century, which suddenly saw a great advance in clock making. Striking clocks, alarm clocks and others that even showed the phases of the moon, the year and the days of the month, were now being made, now that the use of the pendulum in clocks had been discovered.

Galileo had seen that it might be possible to use a pendulum in a clock, and had even carried out a number of experiments with a timepiece with a pendulum attached. But it was left to the Dutch mathematician and astronomer, Christiaan Huygens, to successfully use a pendulum to regulate a clock over a period of time. From then on, it was a comparatively short step to the golden period of clock making that began in the last quarter of the 17th century, when the London clockmakers made their own contribution to the evolution of the clock by designing the longcase clock. The first ones had oaken cases, but when walnut came into favour a few years later, this became the wood most commonly used. The more elegant ones were of the narrow waisted forms of the William and Mary period, with the heads framed with twisted pilasters. Later, the faces were decorated with painted dials of the moon, ships moving on waves, and other conceits.

As there was a wealthy clientele able and only too happy to pay high prices, a number of craftsmen applied their skills to their making, notably Joseph Knibb from Oxford, James Cox of 103, Shoe Lane, London, who also made a perpetual motion clock, and Thomas Tompion, who has been called the father of English clock making, to name just three of the many names in that period of history of clock making. Longcase clocks were also made in Holland and France, the former often heavily embel-

Left: A Louis XIV Long case clock. **Top**: A George III bracket clock. **Above**: An 18th Century Dutch Staartklok.

1

2

1. A Brequet carriage clock.
2. A musical stag clock by
James Cox. 3. An English
18th century carriage clock.
4. A latter day clock by
Gilbert Bayes, dated 1920.
5. A French musical clock
by Stollerwerck of Paris.
6. A timepiece by Joseph
Knibb. 7. A large Meissen
flower encrusted porcelain
clock. 8. A French 'turning
band' clock, representing
Love triumphing over Time.
*Photographs Courtesy of **The
Antique Dealer and
Collector's Guide**.*

6

Late the property of H.R.H. The Duke of Sussex K.G.

From a Model design'd by Prince Rupert.

5

lished with marquetry.

Longcase clocks were not termed grandfather clocks until 1876, when the song 'My Grandfather's Clock' was written.

Soon after the appearance of the longcase clock, bracket clocks began to appear. The term bracket was something of a misnomer, because a large number of them had a handle to them, which meant they could be transported, and could just as easily stand on a table or a mantelpiece.

Bracket clocks were made by all the leading makers of longcase clocks, who had to compete with the imported French carriage clocks, which were more elaborate than those of their English rivals. The influence of French designs in this field cannot be over estimated, as they came to represent an important art form. They were lavishly decorated and imaginative in their conception, even if they seem a little vulgar and ostentatious by today's standards.

About 1850, the French introduced us to the

BOOKS

The Collector's Dictionary of Clocks by H.A. Lloyd.
Old Clocks by H.A. Lloyd.
Watchmakers and Clockmakers of the World by G.H. Baille.
The Longcase Clock by E. Bruton.
The Knibb Family, Clockmakers by R.A. Lee.

MUSEUMS

London: Victoria and Albert Museum, British Museum.
Ibert Collection, Guildhall, Clockmaker's Company Collection.
Bury St. Edmunds, Gershom-Parkington Collection.

carriage clock, which reached its *apogee*, decoratively speaking, some twenty years later. Although a number of fine carriage clocks were made, especially those from the factory of Abraham Louis Brequet, the reputation of French carriage clocks was marred by the introduction of semi mass produced carriage clocks by Paul Garnier, another Parisian clockmaker.

The field of horology is such a vast one that years of study are needed to be devoted to it to understand it fully. But for those who wish merely to collect clocks, the approach must necessarily be different. One aid to buying is that the makers of English 18th century clocks can be identified, as an Act of Parliament forced them to put their names and addresses on their clocks. But even if you have correctly identified a clock, it doesn't mean that it contains all its original parts. It comes back to what is repeated time and time again in this book — go to a specialist dealer.

The valentine vard is said to have taken its name from a bishop named Valentinus, who was made a martyr by the Romans when they put him to death on 14th February AD 270, a date which happened to coincide with the feast of Lupercalia, a heathen fertility feast day. As to why he was chosen to become the patron saint for all lovers remains something of a mystery – especially as the date of 14th February, which is the official date for receiving valentine cards is just as likely to have come from the medieval belief that this was the date when birds mated.

The sending of valentine cards goes back to the 18th century, when it was the custom of lovers to send each other hand written *billet doux*. The first printed valentines appeared in England in 1761, and they bore little resemblance to the highly elaborate cards that were to come later, being little more than a poorly printed sheet with an abominable piece of verse on it. By the turn of the century, it was quite a different story. By then the first English patent for embossing paper had been granted to John Gregory Hancock, and the use of lace paper making had been brought in by Joseph Addenbrooke. With these new facilities to hand, the makers of valentine cards began to produce some beautifully made cards in which red roses, purple flowers and silken hearts were prominently featured.

The sending of valentine cards reached its peak between 1840 and 1870, after the introduction of the Penny Post had further encouraged the sale of something which had already become a craze, leading eventually to more than half a million valentines being sent annually. During this golden period of the valentine card, their makers strived to outdo each other by producing some eye-catching novelty, so extravagantly decorated that it seemed a shame to have to entrust them to some heavy-handed postman.

The quality of many of these valentines could hardly have been bettered, particularly those made by H. Dobbs, 'Ornamental Stationers to the Royal Family', or by Jonathan King, who produced an enormous number of cards in his factory in Islington, London. King amassed a collection of nearly forty thousand cards which he offered to the British Museum, who told him they had no room to house them. After his death, the main bulk of the collection went to America, where the sending of valentine cards had become just as much a craze as it had been in England. The field of the American valentine card is a subject in itself, and much can be read about it in Frank Staff's book, *The Valentine & its Origins,* published by the Lutterworth Press.

The valentine was not used merely as a means of sending anonymous messages of love. Many of them were crude, vulgar and often hurtful, though their use reflected more a part of the British mind that was to respond to the vulgarity of the McGill seaside postcard, rather than a genuine desire to wound.

From the 1880's, the popularity of the valentine declined steadily until 1914, when their production came to an almost complete halt. Fortunately, the custom of sending valentines was revived in the 1920's by the firm of Raphael Tuck, who issued an excellent collection of valentine cards. The sending of valentine cards still remains a popular custom, but the cards today are a very poor imitation of those made in the golden age of the valentine.

FROM YOUR SECRET ADMIRER

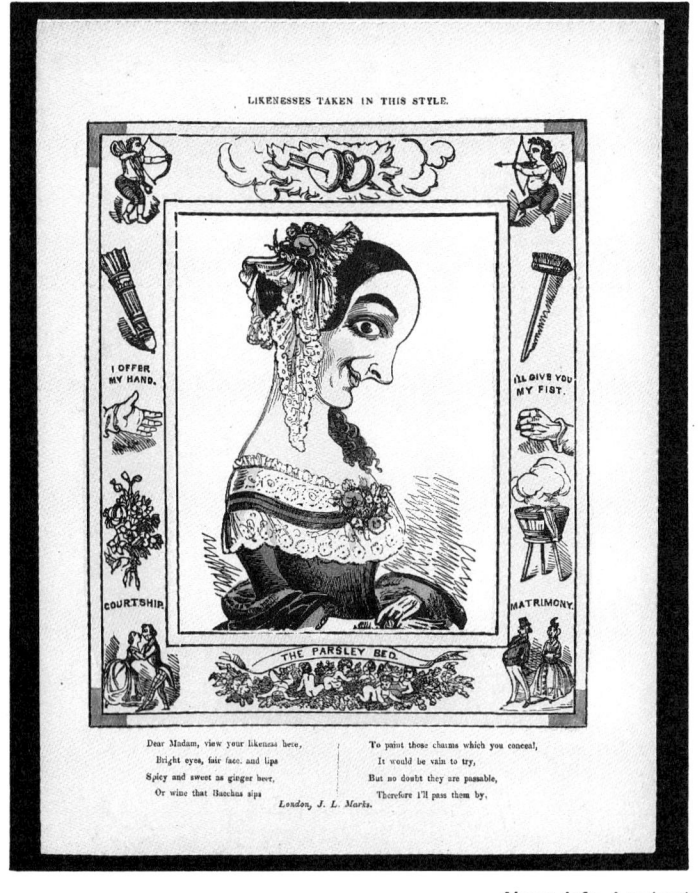

Above left: A valentine card that could have given no pleasure to its recipient.
Above right: A selection of typical valentines from the Victorian period. Pictures Courtesy of **Phillips.**

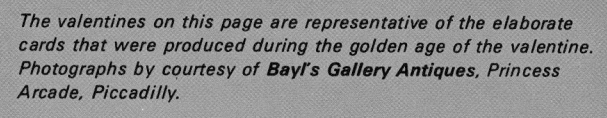

Yesterday's Playthings

Toys were being made as far back as ancient times, but for all practical purposes toy making as an industry did not begin until the 17th century, when Germany began making wooden toys on a massive scale for export.

Although she remained the most famous of all the toy making countries until as late as 1914, by which time she had also begun flooding the market with tin toys, her position had not remained entirely unchallenged. In the early 19th century, Birmingham had become known as 'the toyshop of the world', though most of the toys being produced there were, for the most part, shoddy and ill-made compared to the German toys. France had made a special niche for herself with her working toys, especially those by Fernand Marker, the Dutch had become famous for her

furnishings for doll's houses, the Russians for their nest toys, and the Americans for their Teddy Bears. Britain had become famous for her hollowcast tin soldiers, which Gamages began to sell at the turn of the century, starting with boxed sets of the Life Guards, and ending up with over a hundred different regiments available to collectors. The golliwogs, now considered a racialist toy, was also a purely English toy, even though it looked as if it had been modelled on one of the members of Christie's Nigger Minstrel shows from America.

But the nursery of a prosperous Victorian household reflected mainly the predominance of German toys. In it you were likely to find a Noah's Ark, with thirty two pairs of carved animal figures, a Jack-in-the-Box, a carousel with a small musical movement, and boxes of lead soldiers, probably made either by Georg

Heyde or Johann Carl Fraus of Dresden, who did not receive any serious competition from England until William Britain's Ltd., started making soldiers with a hollow casting instead of using solid lead.

Board games date back to the mid-eighteenth century, and were produced more as an educational tool, rather than as something to amuse a child. Although America made a large number of games during this period, these were for the home market. In England, they were very much a side-line with the toy makers until the nineteenth century, when they suddenly became a large part of the stock of most toy shops. Even then, in one respect the market had not changed a great deal, as the emphasis was still on educational subjects. It was not until the late nineteenth century that games purely for entertainment began to

3

5

4

6

7

appear.

Even after World War I, the Germans were still in the vanguard of toy making with their remarkable range of models of cars, trains and ships, which were remarkable for their detail and accuracy. Some of these toys now fetch hundreds, and sometimes even thousands of pounds in auction room.

But things were beginning to change, as the British toy manufacturers began to compete with the Continental market with their own tinplate toys of cars, planes and ships. Two British companies, Wells and Brinlay were the first pioneers in this field, followed by Chad Valley, who had been operating since 1897, and Hornby's Dinky Toys which began appearing in the shops in 1933. Today, even a fairly recent Dinky Toy fetches a good price in the auction room — something which will no doubt cause some distress to those parents who carelessly consigned them to the dustbin or passed them on, once their own family had grown up. Also highly prized by collectors are the Matchbox series of vintage cars.

8

□ **WHERE TO BUY**
Anthea Knowles Rare Toys,
42 Colebrook Row, N1.
Game Advice, 1 Holmes Road, N1.
Dolls and Toys of Yesteryear,
3-4 Faulkner Square, Charnham,
Hungerford, Berks.

□ **BOOKS**
Tin Toys by Michael Buhler
Nursery Antiques by James MacKay
The Encyclopaedia of Toys by
Constance Eileen King.

1. A mid nineteenth century carved wood butcher's shop.
2. A 1935 Royal Daimler, as supplied to H.M. George V, during his Silver Jubilee Celebrations.
3. Lehmann Chinese porters and swimming seal.
4. German crank operated bare knuckle boxers in ring, circa 1925.
5. Tipp limousine, circa 1920.
6. Chad Valley delivery van, 1940s.
7. Hess battleship, 1920.
8. Goodwin toy of girl with a perambulator, 1868.

PHILLIPS

MAGIC CARPETS

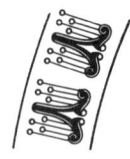

The making of oriental rugs and carpets is one of the least appreciated of the decorative arts. Confined to a comparatively limited area, it is an art executed and refined by generations of anonymous designers and craftspeople over at least 2,500 years.

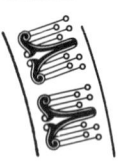

No one can be sure who first came up with the idea of tying woollen knots on to the warp threads of a woven canvas; it is popularly supposed to have been the ancient Persians, though there is perhaps an equally strong case for its having been the ingenious Mongolians. (The oldest surviving rug, the 'Pazyryk' was found frozen in a chieftain's tomb in the Russian steppes and is conservatively dated to about 500 BC). Whoever the inventors were, the technique of making rugs has remained basically unchanged to the present day.

Partly due to Britain's political and trade links with Persia during the 19th century, the vast majority of antique rugs you will find stem from that century when London became established as the rug capital of the world, a status it still retains. However, whilst an age of 100 years is necessary for a rug to be described as 'antique', a considerable degree of leniency is found among dealers and collectors when deciding what is and what is not a worthwhile example. Rugs made as late as the 1930s are still much sought after and, as they are in all essentials made in the same way, with the same materials and designs as older examples, and will be more usable being less worn, they are well worth consideration. (A factor not unworthy of consideration is that rugs from the turn of the century and later will usually cost much less). It is possible to build up a good and representative collection of weaving if one concentrates on fragments, saddle-bags, cushion faces, etc., and does not insist on guaranteed antiquity.

For a decor based on antique furniture there is no floor covering more easily complementary than an oriental rug: the range of design is enormous, from the boldness of tribal pieces such as the Konya, to the ornate opulence of town or city made pieces like the Kirman, and they offer an opportunity for discovery and study which can easily become an absorbing and life-long passion.

Most people starting out will latch on to the rule that a lot of knots to the square inch is a good thing, few knots to the square inch is bad. To a very limited extent this is true. But a good Kazak (tribal) rug of about 100 knots to the inch will usually still be infinitely more attractive and much more valuable than the mediocre Kashan (city rug) with 300 knots to the square inch.

Again, there is much talk about the superiority of vegetable dyes over chemical dyes, and certainly the vegetable dyes used before the

Opposite page. A Khila Carpet (Caucasian) 1860

Above left. Chinese Ning Shia Carpet 1880

Left. Old Indian Amaritzer Carpet 1900

Above. Persian Kirma Carpet circa 1900

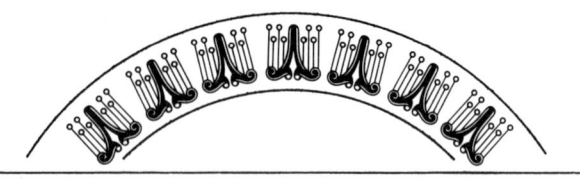

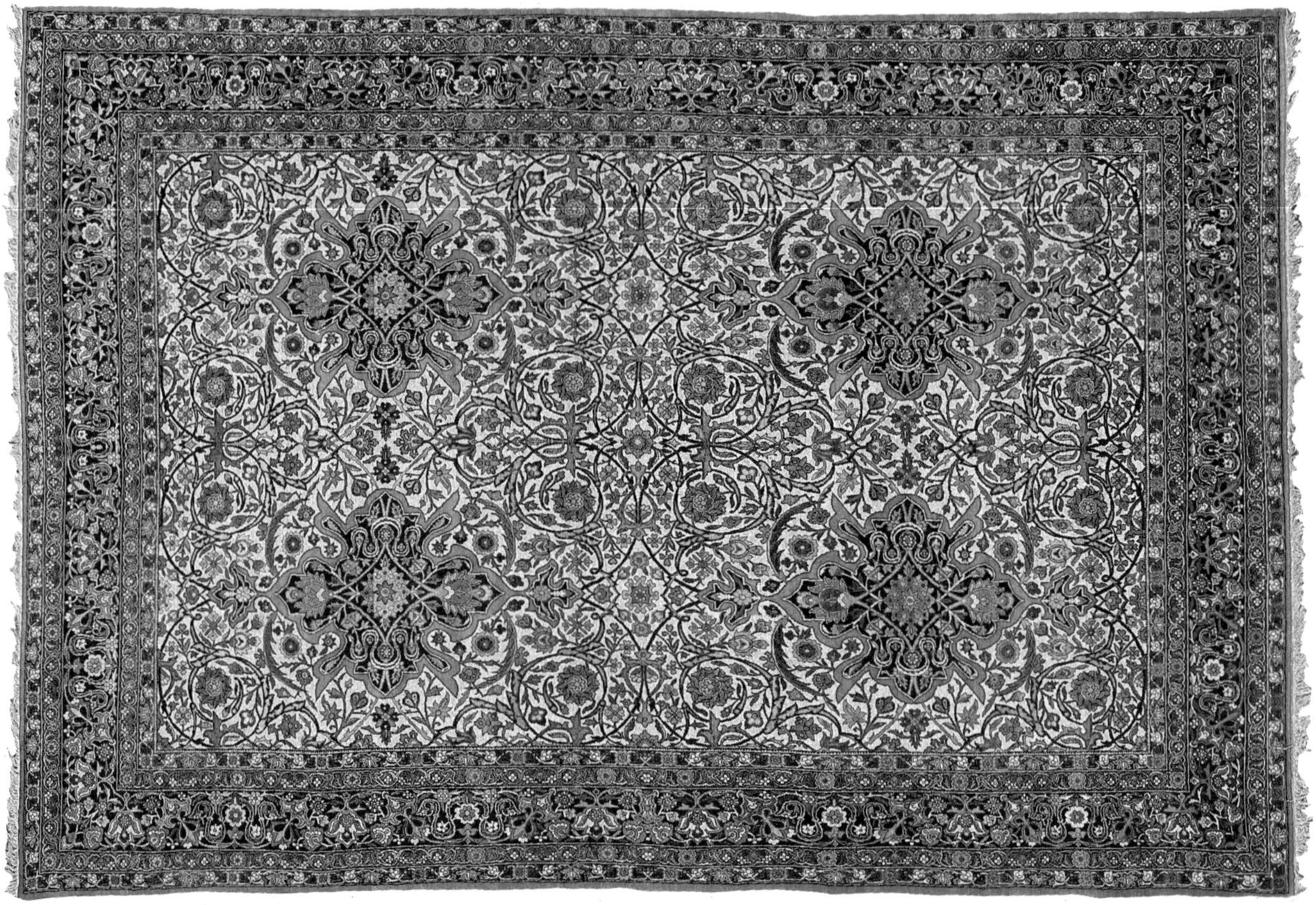

Above. A Turkish Konya Carpet 1890

Right. A Heriz Carpet 1860

invention of synthetic substitutes in the 1880s, do have qualities of depth and subtlety which chemical ones do not achieve. This being said, there are some perfectly hideous vegetable dyed rugs and many exquisite chemically dyed ones. A horrible rug does not become more attractive when it is revealed to be an organically dyed horror.

What determines the value of a rug is a complex equation of age, provenance, condition, rarity and aesthetic quality. Of primary importance is whether or not it is beautiful, but of primary technical importance is the origin of the piece.

Finally, a word of caution: there are a myriad hawkers of rugs, implausible (or perhaps only too plausible) auctioneers of 'liquidated stock' and so forth, who will not be over scrupulous in their sales pitches, nor zealous in correcting your over estimates of a rug's age. In the field of rugs, worn out and tatty means just that: wear does not equal age. Confine your enquiries to reputable dealers, develop a healthy scepticism, grow deaf to such words as 'jewel-like' and avoid 'bargains' like the plague, for like the plague, there hasn't been one for a very long time.

Pictures by courtesy of Vigo Carpet Gallery

Chelsea

PIONEERS IN PORCELAIN

It is not known exactly when the Chelsea Porcelain Factory came into being, but the main body of opinion dates it as 1745, the earliest piece of Chelsea we have with that date on it. This probably makes it the earliest of the six soft paste factories operating in England around that time, as no other porcelain factory's pieces carries an earlier date. As to who owned the factory, this remains something of a mystery. It had been said that the Duke of Cumberland was its patron. But there is no firm evidence to support this.

What we do know is that it began operating on the corner of Lawrence Street, Chelsea, under the management of Charles Gouyn, and that it was then taken over in 1749 by Nicholas Sprimont, who began working for the factory on a salary of a guinea a day. It was during Sprimont's management that the finest and most characteristic pieces of Chelsea porcelain were made.

Sprimont was a Huguenot silversmith who had come to England in 1742, and his background clearly influenced the manner and style of the early Chelsea pieces, as many of their designs showed a close affinity to his silverwork, which made a great use of scrollwork and shell motifs. The early pieces were incised with a triangle.

Probably the most famous of all the Chelsea pieces belonging to that period were the 'goats and bee' jugs, which were supported by two goats, with a twig design for a handle and a porcelain bee on the lip. During that triangle period the decorations consisted mostly of sprays of flowers, leaves and butterflies and insects and exotic plants. Many of the designs were on a plain white background. The factory also produced around this time a number of

Above. Rabbit Tureen, with Red anchor mark. Circa 1755.

Left. Pair of "Chelsea" porcelain groups. These are copies made by Samsons of Paris, who specialised in making copies of early porcelain.

Left. Pair of eel pot vases circa 1758.

The Antique Dealer and Collectors Guide.

Chelsea

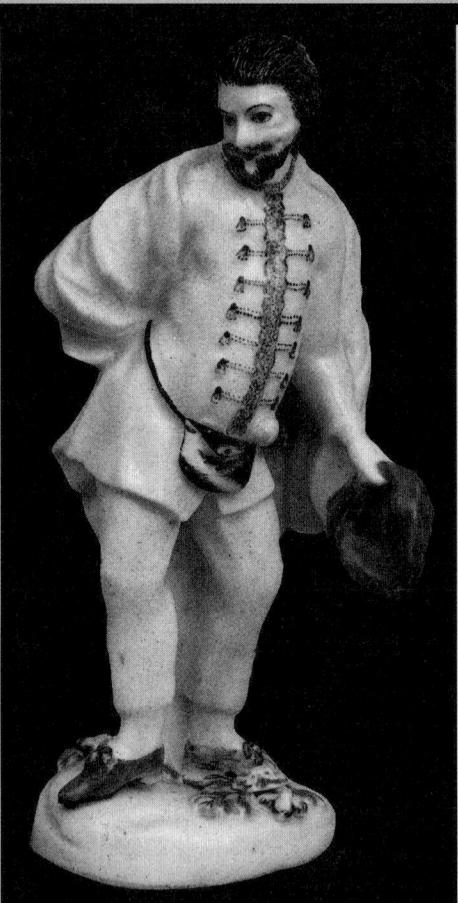

grotesque tea pots which could hardly have been attractive ornaments to have had on the table.

Chelsea's next two periods were known as the red anchor periods, one dating from 1750 to 1753, with an anchor mark placed on a raised medallion, and the other from 1753 to 1758, using a painted anchor, usually accompanied by a triangle of spur marks. The first red anchor period saw the factory taking their designs from a book, *Natural History of Uncommon Birds,* by George Edwards, and from an edition of Aesop's *Fables,* illustrated by Francis Farmer. A third group used figures from Italy's *Commedia dell'Arte,* and a fourth group showed the influence of Meissen pottery. Yet another group drew its inspiration from a series of botanical subjects taken from a number of drawings made by the head gardener at the Chelsea Botanical Gardens. Although neither of these two periods were noted for the originality of their designs, the manner of their execution placed them among the finest works ever to come out of the factory.

The gold anchor mark period dating from 1754 to 1769 saw many changes. Bone ash was now being used in the composition of the paste. Sprimont had taken over the complete control of the factory, and much of the porcelain had now come under the artistic influence of France. Elaborate gilding, rococo scrolls and vibrant colours were all used to give an effect of general magnificence, which was not always in the best of taste. This growing extravagance in the colouring and gilding was accompanied by a corresponding change in the forms of the porcelain itself. But extravagant and bizarre as they sometimes were, they were nevertheless technical triumphs that seemed to set out to show there was nothing a Chelsea potter could not do. Subjects after Watteau and Boucher and other French artists were painted in panels on the vases. Others were painted with curious exotic birds. Following a style set by Dresden, and Chelsea artists festooned the vases with wreaths of flowers, often turning them into what an irreverent layman might call a 'dog's dinner'. Others with a more kindly nature might refer to them merely as examples of misguided

A rare Commedia Dell'Arte figure. Antique Dealer & Collector's Guide.

ingenuity, in which the potter had over-reached himself.

By 1769, Sprimont had made a small fortune for himself from the factory. Having been ill for some time, he decided to sell out and retire to the country. The buyer was William Duesbury, a porcelain decorator who had worked for the Bow and Derby factories before acquiring a controlling interest in the Derby factory. The latter years of Sprimont tenure had seen a deterioration in the previously high standards of the factory. And Duesbury's reign, which began in 1770, did nothing to improve the situation. But at least it was blessed by Duesbury deciding to abandon producing those rococo vases belonging to the last Chelsea period. Less happy was his decision to change the shape of the vases. These new vases were mostly in the classical style, whose only merit lay in the fact that they left large areas of plain space in which a china painter could apply a pleasant landscape or figures. The idea of using a gold stripe decoration instead of a picture, which was to become characteristic of many Derby-Chelsea pieces, turned out to be a happy enough marriage of form and decoration. But others were distinctly unpleasing. The colour was often thin a poor in tone, and in some of the figures a flesh tint was often obtained by a thin wash of red on the exposed parts of the body. More and more of the decorations began to assume the look of Derby porcelain, a company not always known for the excellence of its porcelain.

The end came in 1784, when Duesbury had the kilns and workshops demolished, and the molds either destroyed or removed to his Derby factory, where one suspects his true interests had always lain. It was perhaps not before time, as the original spirit that had made Chelsea such a brilliant pioneer in the field of porcelain, had long since departed

BOOKS

The Red Anchor Wares by F. Severne MacKenna, and *The Gold Anchor Wares* by the same author.

Far left. 3 Botanical Plates. circa 1754-56.
Left. A rare octagonal Bowl. Circa 1752-56.
Sotherbys
Below. Pair of Chelsea Plates. Red Anchor mark. Circa 1756.
The Antique Porcelain Company.

China Fairings

SOUVENIRS FROM THE FAIR GROUNDS

China fairings are very much a part of English social history, although they were made in Germany. Fairings was the name given to a group of brightly coloured hard-paste porcelain ornaments which were sold at fairs, and they give us a very good idea of the sort of humour the Victorians liked, which does not seem to have differed all that greatly from the type of jokes we see on the modern comic seaside card, even if their humour was slightly less ribald.

The comic side of courtship and marriage, drunks, hen-pecked husbands being assailed by their wives with a rolling pin or slipper, and not so hen-pecked husbands being caught *flagrente delicto* by outraged wives, were all popular subjects, as were men leering over a girl's displayed ankle, or being hauled from some hiding place by a girl's irate parents.

Later, children and animals, especially cats, dogs and bears, often dressed in human clothes, began to appear. In contrast to the healthy crudeness of the earlier fairings, these erred on the side of sickly sentimentality.

Some aspects of English social life were also used for fairings. Couples skating, with the female partner showing an amount of leg,

outrageous for the times, or couples having accidents on their boneshakers, or going for coach rides to the races, were also made in large quantities. There was also a line of 'straight' figures of chimney sweeps, bootblacks, servants and street vendors, and a few pieces dealing with scenes from the Franco-Prussian war.

Because the Germans had found a way to produce fairings more cheaply than anyone else, they were able to monopolise the market. To begin with, they were made by Conta and Boehme, who were supplied with captions and rough sketches to work from by the English distributors.

When shops eventually began to sell them, however, other German makers began to produce fairings which were more crude than those produced by Conta and Boehme. Attempts were made to market them in France and Germany, with translated captions, but they were a failure, as their humour was so essentially English.

Fairings departed from the scene somewhere about 1890. Fortunately for us, so many were made that there is still no difficulty in picking up pieces, often at reasonable prices.

Above. A fairing titled **Fish Cleaning**.

Top right. Useful fairings: The Puss in boot is a pin box, the bird and cat a jam pot, the bear a mustard pot, and the pugs, pepper and mustard containers, with a basin for salt.

Middle. The girl with a lamb and the standing boy are match strikers, the boy with a dog a trinket box.

Bottom Right. Three typical Conta and Boehme fairings.

Antique Dealer and Collector's Guide

MUSEUMS

London: The Victoria and Albert Museum. Most museums will have at least a few examples of china fairings on display. For detailed information on fairings read:
Victoria China Fairings
by
William S. Bristowe.

The power of love.

Five o'clock Tea.

Returning at one o'clock in the morning.

All antiques express the personality and tastes of the person who made them. In the case of the sampler, the clever needlework of some little girl from the 18th or 19th century tells us as much about her as one of her exercise books would have done.

The decorative art of

SAMPLERS

To begin with, samplers were needlework panels executed by young girls as an exercise in practising various stitches, worked up in simple patterns with coloured silks on a piece of coarse linen.

The earliest existing examples date from the beginning of the 17th century, and generally feature birds, flowers and letters of the alphabet. Nearly always, the name of the child who made the sampler was added as a final touch when the work was completed.

The art of making samplers soon became part of the education of every well brought up girl to turn her into a skilled needlewoman. Many were taught from the age of five.

The art of the sampler flourished particularly in Victorian times, when many very young girls were taught needlework, with many of the samplers being signed by girls of seven or eight. Sampler-making became part of the curriculum of many schools, who used them to help teach a child its alphabet and numbers — thereby seeing to it that a child was learning two subjects at once.

Considering the age of the children, these apprentice pieces show a skill that is hardly believable by modern standards. But then perhaps this was not really so surprising when one learns that the children were taught everything from plain sewing and mending and simple decorative stitching, to the most elaborate forms of stitches.

As with everything else with the Victorians, children were taught with a thoroughness that is often sadly lacking in many of our schools today. Even so, it is interesting to note that as late as when television was in its infancy, Odham's part work, "Wonderland of Knowledge", was still able to devote a whole page in dense type on 'How to Make a Sampler'.

But not all samplers were merely exercises for children. Young ladies of leisure started passing the time by learning to become fine

Above. An early 19th century sampler by Agnes Phin, aged 12, 1828, with pious verse and alphabet.

PHILLIPS

needlewomen, using the sampler for their exercise pieces. Experts were often employed in some of the great houses to teach the craft. Indeed, many of them often moved from house to house, and even from country to country, as the making of samplers became more and more a popular recreational activity. The more popular it became, the more new stitches and designs were sought after.

Nothing became too difficult for them. Cross and satin stitches, with floral borders of the most elaborate kind, were done as a matter of course, as was the Map Sampler, which was often an extremely complicated map worked in outline with black silk.

The themes covered a vast range of subjects. Adam and Eve and the Serpent, under a tree bearing an apple, canvases teeming with figures and houses, shepherds and shepherdesses and their sheep, and long pieces of biblical texts or extracts from some of the more popular poems of the day, were all executed with a staggering degree of professionalism.

The craft of the sampler was very far from

being confined to this country. The Dutch introduced the Darning Sampler, which were samplers worked in darning stitches, and crammed with animals, birds and flowers. The Spanish gave us samplers done in vivid colours, and samplers were also produced in Germany and Mexico.

But it in was America that the sampler really thrived more than anywhere else, thanks mainly to the English families who had immigrated to New England. The earliest existing ones came from Salem, Massachussetts, and are very like the samplers that were being produced in England at the same time.

A different trend appeared in America in the latter part of the 18th century, when genealogical samplers began to appear, giving not only the dates of birth, marriages and deaths in a family, but also listing whole family trees.

But interesting though these might be, they lack the charm of many of the early English samplers executed by little girls learning to sew. The very earliest sampler still in existence, incidentally, is dated 1643, and is to be found in the Victoria and Albert museum, South Kensington.

One of the interesting things about the Victorian samplers is their preoccupation with death. This was something the Victorian child was taught to live with at a very early age — perhaps with some justification, as the mortality rate among children was very high. Nevertheless, pious exhortations to Gentle Jesus to take their little soul to His Heavenly Kingdom, could not have cheered a child, as she did her sampler exercise, which must have made her wonder sometimes if she was going to be able to complete her sampler before being called.

Buying Samplers

As to the collecting of samplers, they are easily enough found, and many of them can be bought at reasonable prices, although their condition does vary greatly. Obviously, the type to look for are samplers that show technical merit. Because 17th century samplers are very rare and can really only be seen in museums, the collectors will have to look for Victorian samplers. The more rare items include the map samplers, which are somewhat lacking in charm, and the commercial samplers, made mainly for the hosery trade. There are even puzzle samplers around. But these again are not really the type you want to have on your wall simply for the pleasure of looking at them.

The simple but often charming ones done by children are the easiest to find. You will find many of them framed, so obviously you have to look out for woodworm. Grimy samplers abound, but these can be salvaged, as they can be cleaned with water and a detergent on a flat surface. But if the sampler shows even the slightest signs of rotting, on no account try cleaning it with anything else but potato flour, which will remove some of the grime, if the flour is applied several times, and then carefully brushed off after each application. The obvious answer, though, is to buy one in perfect condition, if possible.

Below. A mid-18th Century needlework sampler by Ann Knapp, 1769, the wool ground embroidered in coloured silks.

It has been said that the print is the poor man's painting. Although this is true to some extent, inasmuch that a large number of quite old prints can be bought inexpensively, it is still hardly appropriate to apply it to a field where literally thousands of pounds can change hands for a single print.

If one concentrated on the 18th century English prints alone, the range of subjects to choose from is enormous. You have the choice of collecting sporting prints, topographical prints, or prints depicting historical events. Then there are the prints of the horse artists and the prints of the caricature artists such as Rowlandson, Gilfaray and Hogarth, to say nothing of all those prints of birds which can be found time and time again in portfolios or already framed, in practically every antique shop in the land. If one extended the field to include foreign prints, such as the Napoleonic prints of Meissonier and the Piranesi prints of Roman views, the choice becomes almost staggering. It is therefore probably best to concentrate on the works of the English artists of the 18th and 19th century.

The most obvious choice for anyone not wanting to spend too much on prints is George Baxter (1804-67) a wood engraver who produced a large number of excellent prints, the most famous of them probably being *The*

THE POOR MAN'S PAINTINGS

Opening of Queen Victoria's Parliament. When the patent expired on a special process he had invented which involved using sometimes more than a dozen wood or metal blocks for a single colour print, one of the licencees of the process was Abraham Le Blond, a highly collectable artist, whose most characteristic prints were small ovals of rustic scenes. *The Cherry Seller,* which we illustrate above, is a typical Le Blond print, which belongs to a set of 32 ovals.

For Topographical prints one could perhaps look for the work of the Brothers Samuel and Nathan Buck, who produced a series of topographical prints between 1728 and 1749, when they completed the mammoth task they had set themselves of producing more than 80 panoramas of cities and towns throughout the whole of England and Wales. Another artist to keep in mind for topographical prints is Paul Sandby, who began producing aquatints in 1775. His work, though, is not easy to come by, but sometimes his views of Windsor and Warwick Castle can be found. If you find the prices of these too heady for your liking, there are many other prints available by lesser known artists, whose work can be had at reasonable prices.

Racing and sporting prints were produced in large quantities during the 18th century. Apart from George Stubbs, who painted all the

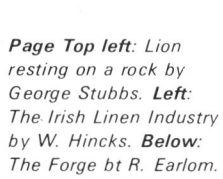

*Page Top left: Lion resting on a rock by George Stubbs. **Left**: The Irish Linen Industry by W. Hincks. **Below**: The Forge bt R. Earlom.*

leading horses of his day as well as producing large numbers of animal prints, one could also include John Sartorius, one of the most prolific horse artists of his time, Samuel Howitt, who published a set of line engravings covering every field of sport, and George Morland, who, although noted mainly for his sentimental scenes of farmyard and domestic life, also produced a whole range of prints on a wide range of sporting subjects.

Obviously it would help the collector if he knew a little of the various processes used in the making of prints. We have therefore appended a short list of useful books worth studying.

BOOKS
Collecting Prints by Brian Allen
How to Identify Old Prints by F.L. Wilder
Aquatint Engraving by S.T. Prideaux
Collecting Pictures by Guy R. Williams

MUSEUMS
Most museums have at least a small collection of 18th century prints. Larger collections may be seen at
The British Museum
The London Museum
National Maritime Museum, Greenwich

Acquiring an eye for ART

U nlike collecting watercolours, an area where it is still possible to buy an attractive picture at a reasonable price, oils are somewhat more difficult to come by, if you are not intending to spend several thousand on a picture. It is, of course, easy enough to pick up some daub gathering dust in a junk shop, where you have been lured by all those stories that have been circulated of priceless masterpieces being picked up for a song in such places. It *has* happened, but the odds against you are so high that you would be far better employed in going straight to dealer.

As with watercolours, the field of the 19th century painters is the best area to explore. If you are looking for something merely as a piece of furnishing, portraits, especially if they are of some unknown person, can be bought cheaply. The portrait of an attractive woman, not unnaturally, will fetch more than one of some respectable worthy whose uneventful life is reflected in every line of his face.

Marine painting can sometimes be bought at a reasonable price, as long as it is not by major artists like Charles Napier Hemy or Henry Redmore, whose pictures have fetched prices running into many thousands. Small rural and coastal scenes can also be found that will not make too much of a hole in your resources. However, genre pictures, at one time thought to be *kitsch,* now fetch fancy prices. Prices, though can fluctuate enormously depending on current trends with artists. Unfortunately, for the buyer, at least, the Victorian painters have become much more collectable lately, so don't expect too much in the way of bargains.

By and large the best approach is to find yourself a reliable dealer with whom you can strike up some sort of relationship. He will value you if you become a good customer, and will put the odd picture your way, well below its marked price, especially if he has some unsold pictures left over from a recent exhibition.

Although the Antiques Club at Woodbridge have produced a number of valuable guides to artists, very little has been published on what to look for in the way of pictures. A book well worth getting on the subject, however, is How To Buy Pictures, by Huon Mallalieu, one of Christie's Collector's Guides.

WHERE TO BUY

David Cross (for marine paintings) Bristol, Avon.

The Cotswold Galleries, Stow-on-the-Wold, Glos.

Mandells Gallery, Norwich.

The Priory Gallery, Cheltenham.

E. Stacey Marks, Eastbourne.

1. **Ploughing** *by Arthur Spooner 24" x 36"*
2. **Still Life** *by Oliver Clare 15" x 18"*
3. **Roasting Chestnuts** *by Edouard Frere 10" x 12½"*
4. **Two Quays – Mevagissey** *by Gyrth Russell 20" x 30"*
5. **By the Seaside** *by Edward Atkinson Hornel 14" x 10"*
6. **Springtime** *by William K. Blacklock 18" x 24"*
7. **Rather Shy** *by Henry Weigas 28" x 36" R.A. Exhibit 1890*
8. **Interesting News** *by Haynes King 18" x 24"*

Photographs by Courtesy of:
The Priory Gallery – Cheltenham.

6

7

8

Inexpensive

Above. *an abundance of hearts: Silver heart-shaped frame. French black and white enamel theometer, registering the 'degrees of love'. Heart shaped pottery inkwell, circa 1860. Silver toast rack with heart shaped holders. Heart shaped papier mache box, embossed with mother of pearl. A two handed Staffordshire loving cup. 19th century Scottish Paisley scarf with heart motif.*
Antiquarus Antique Centre

COLLECTABLES

There are quite a lot of people who would like to have small antiques around them which do not cost an arm and a leg to buy. For these sensible souls, small dealers and especially the antique markets are the first stopping off points.

Most of the large markets carry a staggering array of stock, covering the whole range of small antiques. In the markets there is generally a more flexible attitude towards prices. Almost any dealer anywhere will give you 10% (when asked). With a stall holder in the markets, you're likely to do even better, as long as you don't keep saying, "but what is your *lowest* price," which is liable to make the stall holder very unhappy indeed.

Yet another advantage of the antique markets

is that you can wander from stall to stall without being bothered, unlike in many of the small antique shops, where the owner, who has probably had a bad day, tends to hover in the background, ready to pounce if you show the slightest interest in anything.

On the other hand, the small markets that are set up for one day in the month in some village or church hall are somewhat of a waste of time, as a great deal of the stock is mere bric-a-brac, and often overpriced at that.

But what do you buy, which satisfies both your love of beautiful things and your desire to possess something which is going to increase its value with the passage of time? There are no hard and fast rules here. In certain areas, prices are not likely to increase much, while in

others, the prices suddenly rocket, sometimes merely because television has done a programme on them. A particular example is the pottery painted by Clarice Cliff, who was a director of both the Newport and Royal Staffordshire potteries, and was still working until 1939. Her bold and brightly coloured designs were considered somewhat passe until quite recently. A two part television programme on her work further added to her reputation, so that pottery pieces painted by her have now gone up in price enormously.

Lacemaker's bobbins, small silver, watches, Victorian jewellery, decanters and certain pieces of glassware can still be had at reasonable prices. As you can see from the few illustrations here, the range is almost endless.

Below: *A large Victorian scrap.*

Right: *Hand coloured antique aquatint of Camelleas. Painted glass/brass firescreen. Flower embroidered Victorian net dress trimming. 'Floral Wealth' in Berlin woodwork. Tulips on beaded bag.*

Below Right: *Some period fashion accessories.*

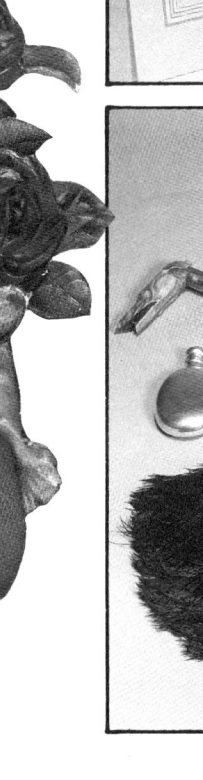

The term 'Staffordshire', when applied to pottery, covers the various types of ware that came out of the five towns of the Potteries between the 18th and 19th century. They were either salt glazed or lead glazed, and were produced for people with modest incomes who wanted something for their mantelpiece at a price they could afford.

The pioneers in the field of producing cottage style ornaments were John Astbury and Thomas Whieldon, whose pieces now fetch thousands in the auction rooms. Astbury's reputation was made when he improved the clays used by the Staffordshire potters by introducing calcined flints in the clay. Thomas Whieldon, probably the most important of the Staffordshire potters, became well known for his tortoise-shell glaze, which was obtained by blending metallic oxides in a clear lead glaze, and are always referred to as 'Astbury-Whieldon' pieces. (see picture left which is an extremely rare and highly important Astbury-Whieldon Tea Party Group).

Although many of the Staffordshire potters were anonymous figures working away in tiny backstreet factories, a few notable names have emerged. These include Obadiah Sherratt, an ale-house keeper and a part time potter who produced some rather bizarre groups, including *The Death of Monro,* which shows a Lieutenant Hector Monro of the Bengal Lancers about to have his head bitten off by a black tiger, and a range of equally unpleasant bull baiting pieces, for some obscure reason a popular subject with a number of the Staffordshire potters. By

Pair of figures of a Ram and Ewe, circa 1770. **Sotherby's.**

A group of attractive Staffordshire figures. **Chenil Galleries, Chelsea.**

Top. A Ralph Wood Senior bull baiting group.
Above. A British Admiral.

contrast, Sherratt's *Polito's Menagerie* is a rather charming piece, showing some of the animals that were in Polito's travelling menagerie, which had no doubt come to Sherratt's attention when it toured the Potteries in 1808.

But the most famous of all the potters was the Wood family, consisting of Ralph Wood the Elder, and his son Ralph, and Aaron the brother of the Elder, who had their factory in Burslem, where they created all manner of pieces of Staffordshire pottery. Sometimes working from models made by the sculptor, John Voyez, who seems to have been drunk more often than he was sober. Ralph Wood Senior made a number of Toby Jugs and group pieces, including his famous Dozing Parson and his Clerk, an undoubtedly well made but hideously vulgar piece to have on a mantelpiece, one would have thought. He also produced an equally famous elephant teapot, some bull baiting pieces and a number of fine equestrian figures. Ralph II, who inherited the factory after his father's death in 1840, is remembered for using enamel to cover his figures, but, generally speaking, his work is not up to the standard set by his father. Aaron was a modeller who had worked for a number of Staffordshire potters, including Whieldon, before going into business with the rest of the family. He made a number of pieces for the Wood factory before moving on to join Josiah Wedgwood at his Ivy House Works in Burslem, where Wedgwood was to make his reputation and become Potter to the Queen.

Because all the work of the above mentioned potters is now so expensive to buy, it is mostly the work of the anonymous Staffordshire potters whose groups and figures have become familiar, even to those who know nothing about antiques. These popular figures are charming in their way, and the most familiar ones to be seen around are those of dalmatians, deer, King Charles spaniels, greyhounds and zebras. That there are so many of these around is hardly surprising as there are an enormous number of fakes on the market.

But even better known are the Staffordshire portrait figures, who represent the prominent figures of their time in about every field you can think of. Boxers, cricketers, politicians and preachers, Queen Victoria and Albert, Garibaldi and Lord Nelson and Dick Turpin, and even the occasional murderer were just a few of the subjects the Staffordshire potters used as their models.

To begin with the figures were moulded, but as time went by the Staffordshire potters began using press moulding, thereby producing figures whose backs were flat and were meant to be viewed from only one side. By producing them in this way the price was kept down. The colours were unsophisticated, and much use was made of a vivid cobalt blue. But at least they made a jolly ornament to have on the mantelpiece, and because they were cheap and cheerful, they were immensely popular.

For their reference the potters went mostly to old prints for their historical subjects, and to steel engravings in newpapers for their contemporary subjects. Occasionally, in the case of singers, they went to music sheets, which often carried a picture of the singer who had made a piece so popular.

Although the pieces were identified with the model's name in gilt on the base, they are not always easily identifiable, as in many cases the gilt has been rubbed off with the passing of time. A further complication is that if a model did not do well, its subsequent issues went out with a new name on them!

The Staffordshire potters were, for the most part, simple and untroubled people who saw their subjects with a child-like eye, which led them to producing a form of primitive folk art

which has a freshness and charming simplicity about it, which a more sophisticated potter could never hope to emulate.

As has already been indicated, there are fakes galore on the market, many of them made recently. These can be spotted by their lightness and a far too even overall crazing to give them an appearance of age. This fake crazing can be spotted with the aid of a strong magnifying glass, as the crazing has invariably been put on with a very fine brush. As if this was not enough to contend with, there are also the Samson of Paris reproductions, which are not so easy to spot, and are the bane of the not too well informed collectors of porcelain in any field.

Despite all the pitfalls for the collector of Staffordshire figures, they have at least the consolation that genuine Staffordshire figures can still be bought at reasonable prices, often well under £100.

BOOKS

Staffordshire Chimney Ornaments by Reginald Haggar

Staffordshire Pottery Figures by Sir Herbert Read.

Staffordshire Portrait Figures by John Hall.

Early Staffordshire Pottery by Bernard Rackham.

Staffordshire Portrait Figures of the Victorian Age by Thomas Balston.

MUSEUMS

London: Victoria and Albert Museum.
Brighton: Art Gallery and Museum.
Canterbury: Royal Museum.
Stoke-on-Trent: City Museum and Art Gallery.
Melton Mowbray: The Balston Collection, Stapleford Park House.

DEALERS

Chenil Galleries, Chelsea, at Unit 3-4.
Woodstock Antiques, 11 Market Street, Oxon.
Godden of Worthing, 17-19 Crescent Road, Worthing, Sussex.

Top left. Tom Sayers & Heeman, who fought on 17th April 1860. Top right. A Staffordshire pair of cricketers. Above. A rare salt glaze Pew Group.

Antique Dealer & Collectors Guide.

Nailsea Glass

Nailsea coloured glass is one of the few areas in the field of antiques where prices have not shot up enormously over the last few years. This is rather surprising because much of it is very attractive to look at as well as being a very decorative object to have around the house.

Its production has always been associated with the village of Nailsea, some eight miles outside Portsmouth, where John Robert Lucas established a glass works in 1788. The business, while it lasted, was obviously a prosperous one, because in addition to the glass works Lucas built nineteen cottages for his employees. But actually what we refer to as Nailsea today did not necessarily come from Nailsea, as much of it was made in places like Stourbridge, Newcastle, Warrington, Castleford, and even from as far afield as a glass works in Alloa, in Scotland. Nailsea is therefore a term which refers to a style, rather

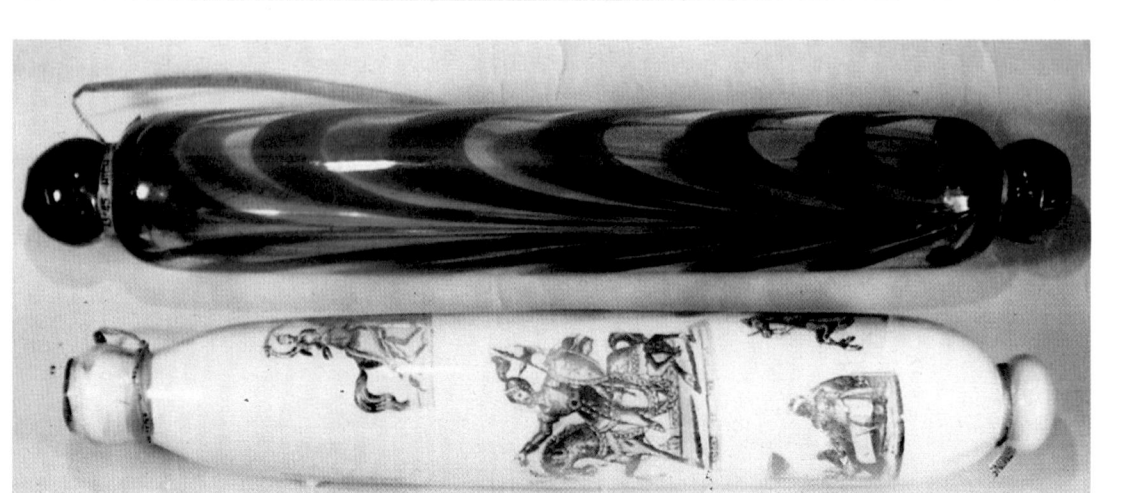

Above. Crown glass carafe with coloured splashes. Circa 1860.

Top left. Blue opaline rolling pin with blue looping. Circa 1870. *Below it*, another plain blue rolling pin of the same date.

Bottom left. Two rolling pins. Circa 1870. The bottom one is chalk filled.

Top Right. Three distinctive and attractive bells.

than the actual place of origin. It is, moreover, virtually impossible to tell where a piece of Nailsea came from, as all of them are unmarked.

When Lucas went into partnership with his brother-in-law, Edward Homer, and William Chance in 1793, the factory was producing crown window glass in large quantities. The pale green in which it appeared was dictated by necessity rather than choice, as to have produced a clear flint glass would have placed it in the luxury category, thereby subjecting it to iniquitous Excise Glass Tax that was always higher than on plain glass.

This unhappy state of affairs for the glass makers and public alike, lasted until 1850, when the glass tax was lifted, after it had dawned on the powers-that-be that the tax was crippling the glass making industry which, hitherto had been forced to compete with the continental glass makers, who had now firmly established themselves throughout the whole of Europe. The removal of the tax was to act as a great spur to the British glass industry, which was soon to see a great boom with its wares.

Not that the tax had entirely stifled the inventiveness of the Nailsea glass blowers. Even before 1800 glass was being produced that was decorated with a trailing white ornamentation, or decorated even more attractively with blue, white and pink stripes. After the tax had been removed, even more ambitious forms of decoration were used to enhance the beauty of the object. Sometimes *latticino* was used. This was an Italian process from Venice, going back to the early part of the 16th century, in which glass was decorated by embedding canes of white opaque glass within a piece of white or coloured glass.

Above. Left to right: Wine carafe. A bell with a clear glass handle and an ornamental bellows with a conical foot.

Below: A bottle of red striated glass. Late 18th or early 19th century.

Opposite page: A pipe decorated in opaque white, pink and blue, and below it — a bottle of clear glass with dark blue striations. Late 18th or early 19th century.

Top Far right: A typical Nailsea jug, Circa 1820, and below it — a flask in the form of a pair of bellows, with looped striations in pink and white enamel, early 19th century.

Pictures throughout by Courtesy of **Somervale Antiques**

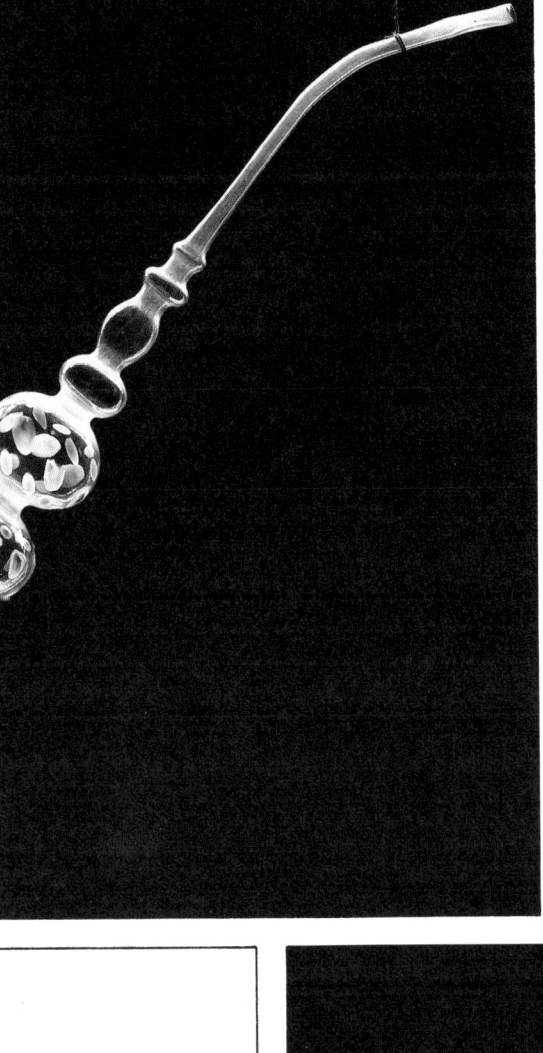

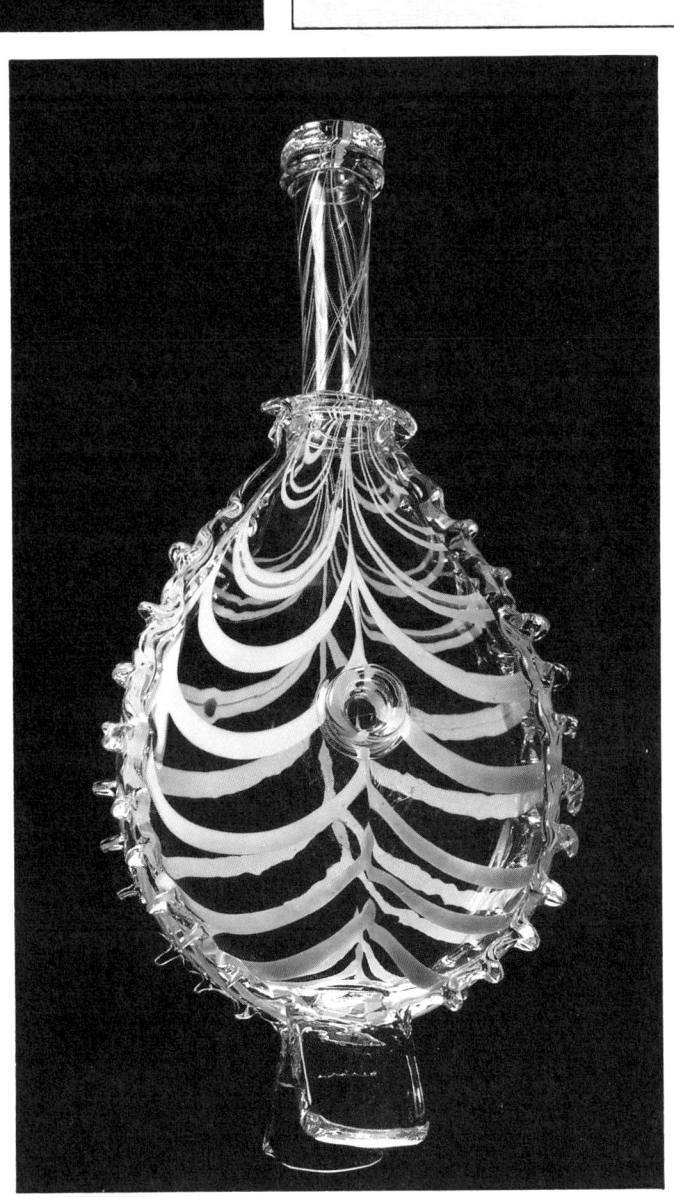

Spatter ware was also produced in large quantities. This was a type of opaque white or coloured glass lined in white with the exterior mottled with large spots in different colours. This idea, developed at the original Nailsea factory was later adopted and produced in large quantities in America.

An interesting aspect of the making of Nailsea glass was the production of novelty items known as friggers, which were made by the glass blower in his own time, or on his day off. These consisted of a large range of charming items, including miniature glass walking sticks, bells, bugles, little glass shoes, figures of animals and ships, and a somewhat less than charming glass tadpole which remained whole however hard you struck it, until you tapped it on the tail, when it promptly shattered into pieces.

There were also the 'dumpies', or door stops, which were made mostly in the North, where they were turned out as individual pieces rather than being made as an after-thought from left-over pieces of glass. A form of dumpies was produced as late as the 1920s, with 'raindrops' or bubbles in them. But interesting as they are, they can hardly be called collector's pieces, and should therefore be avoided if you are thinking seriously of collecting Nailsea.

Another interesting novelty were the Nailsea pieces of glass shaped in the form of a pipe which were often used as shop signs outside tobacconists and as tavern ornaments.

Glass factories throughout the country were not slow to see that there was a very large potential market in the production of friggers, and a number of them, particularly those at Stourbridge, Alloa, and of course, Nailsea, began to mass produce them — which is one of the reasons why so many of them are still to be

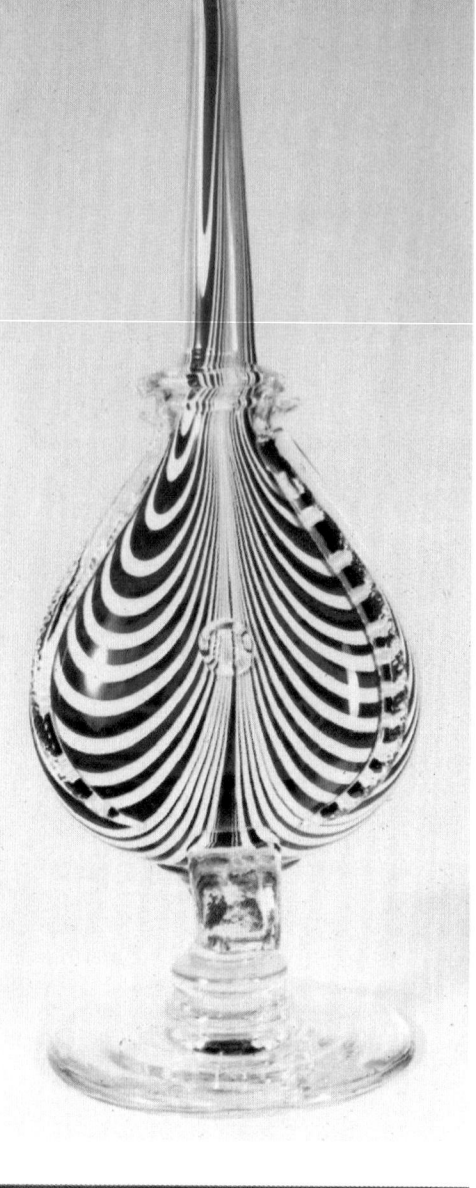

found from one end of England to the other.

One of the most popular of all the friggers were the rolling pins, probably because they could be put to a practical use as well as being decorative. They came in a number of colours and were often produced as commemorative pieces, or with little scenes on them. Most of them also carried some form of legend or a motto on them. Others were engraved with naval subjects, depicting frigates, compasses and famous admirals. It is interesting to note, incidentally, how Britain's naval inheritance was so often used as a subject to decorate so many forms of popular antiques, such as the Stevengraphs, Valentines, and the Stafford-shire mantle pieces.

Their popularity was so enormous that they were often given as wedding or christening gifts. Quite often they were borne triumphantly home as a souvenir from some seaside resort. Considering they were mass produced for a popular market, the glass used for them was of a surprisingly high quality. These delightful items were produced mainly between 1830 and 1860, but as was so often the way with things produced for a large scale in those days, their popularity waned suddenly, and long before the beginning of the next century they had become almost a part of English social history.

What examples of Nailsea should one buy? Obviously the condition of the item is of vital importance. In the case of the rolling pins, a number can be found where the pattern has been partially worn away and could not, therefore, be classified as a desirable item. Many of the other types of Nailsea are in a poor condition, which is another reason why there are so many of them around. Dealers, especially those from America or the Conti-nent, leave them severely alone, and they generally end up on some stall in one of the smaller antique markets. A good rolling pin will fetch anything from £40 to £100, whereas a rolling pin in a poor condition can be had for

something less than £20 – if you must insist on buying something which is certainly not going to rise in value, even with the passage of time.

The Nailsea glass bells are not so easily found, especially if they are in good condition. A plain coloured glass bell will fetch some-thing in the region of £80, others decorated with some sort of design, like a fleur de lys pattern, from £150. As with eveything in life, you get what you pay for unless you are exceptionally lucky.

As you can see, there is not an enormous variation in prices, which makes this a field in which a collection can be built up for a relatively reasonable sum. It has not been our policy in this book to go into prices, but in the case of Nailsea glass, we feel we can give you a fair approximation, as it seems unlikely they will go up very much in the near future.

Where do you buy? Nailsea glass is not the sort of thing that turns up very often in the major auction houses, and is therefore much more likely to be found in the small antique shop or in one of the antiques centres or markets. We know of only one dealer who really specialises in Nailsea glass, whose address is given below.

WHERE TO BUY

Somervale Antiques, 6 Radstock Road, Midsomer Norton, Bath. Shop open only by appointment, but has a twenty four hour telephone service (0761) 412686.

BOOKS

Nailsea Glass by Keith Vincent. The one and only book dealing, as far as we know, with the subject of Nailsea glass.

MUSEUMS

The Municipal Museum, Warrington.
Gilchrist Collection, Cowes, Isle of Wight.

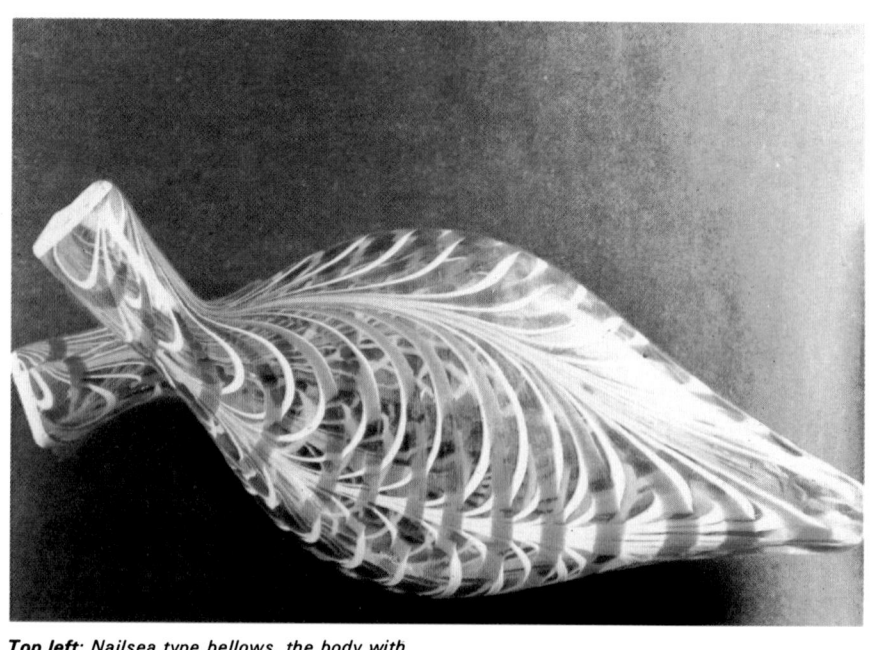

Top left: Nailsea type bellows, the body with opaque white and red looping, rib moulded sides on a plain stem with conical foot. Circa 1860.

Left: A Nailsea pipe. Circa 1860.

Above: A gimmel flask. Circa 1860.

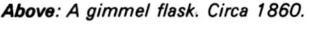

STUDIES IN SILK
THE ART OF THE STEVENGRAPH

S tevengraphs was a trade name the Coventry weaver Thomas Stevens used to describe the silk woven articles which he produced in his recently acquired Jacquard looms. The loom had been invented in France in 1801, and it was to revolutionise the textile industry because it could weave highly complicated patterns and needed only one man to operate it. Both Stevens and another weaver named John Caldicott were the first to see the potential for creating a new market with the Jacquard loom, and in fact, Caldicott was the first one to register the design for a bookmarker ribbon. But it was Stevens who was to

Right: *An early Stevens silk bookmarker.*
Below: *A silk picture from Stevens' naval series.*

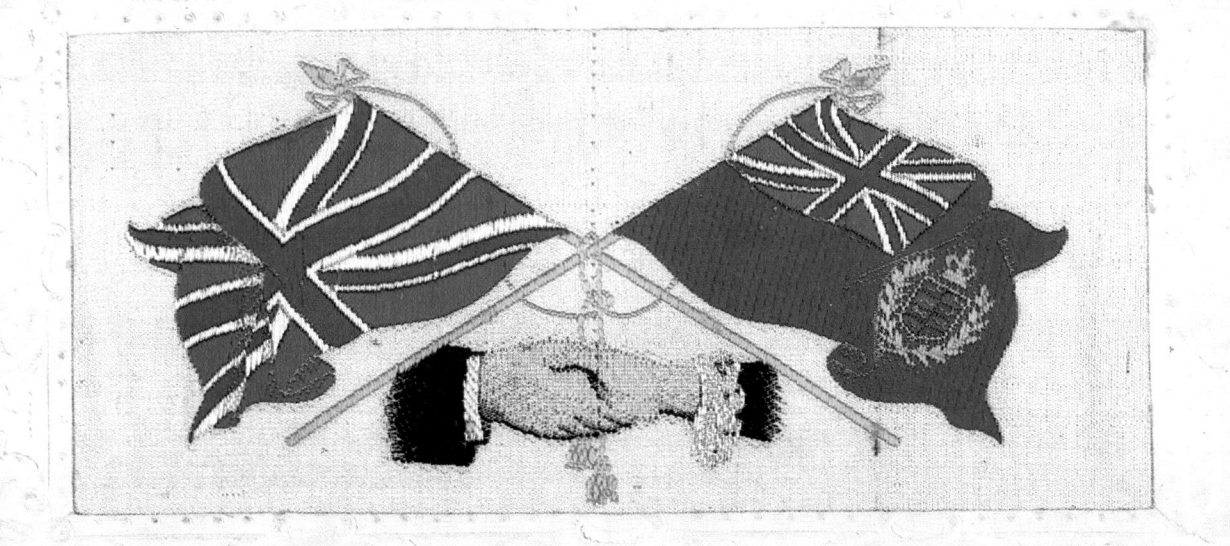

HANDS ACROSS THE SEA.

WOVEN IN SILK

R.M.S. CALGARIAN.

exploit this new market to the full, when he began producing his own bookmarkers in 1862.

Weaving silk ribbons was not something new to Coventry, which as an industry, had begun about 1700, only to collapse in 1860, when the government revoked its prohibition of imported silks, leaving the way clear for France to begin sending in countless miles of silk ribbons at highly competitive prices. Rather than trying to compete with them in this field, Stevens adapted his looms to weave an upright design rather than a horizontal and continuous one. After they had come off the machines, Stevens simply cut them in short strips and then sold them as bookmarkers to booksellers and stationers, who were delighted to stock this new line, which made an attractive and inexpensive present. Stevens claimed to have made over nine hundred different subjects for them, ranging from bible markers with an appropriate piece of religious text, to bookmarkers designed to be used as a valentine.

Even so, Stevens' hour did not really come until he had demonstrated his looms at a York Exhibition in 1879. Here, for the first time he produced his new brainchild — the Stevengraph picture.

His first two subjects were carefully chosen; Dick Turpin's Ride to York, accompanied by a sentimental piece of verse paying homage to the bravery of his horse, Black Bess, and the

---

Below: A silk picture from Stevens' naval series.

London to York Stage Coach, which had commenced running in 1706.

Stevens had already become something of a household name with his bookmarkers. Now he had created an entirely new market, where people began collecting his silk pictures as souvenirs. Silk pictures on almost any subject you could think of, poured from his looms at the rate of a new subject every month. There were his landscape views which included the Crystal Palace, the Tower of London, the Houses of Parliament and Balmoral Castle. Then there was his historical scenes which covered such best sellers as Grace Darling's Life Boat Rescue, the Death of Nelson, and the Lady Godiva Procession. To list even a fraction of the subjects he covered would make tedious reading. It is sufficient to say that he produced literally hundreds of different Stevengraphs. Many were designed for selling in America, where they became almost as popular as they were in this country.

Stevens died in 1888, but the firm continued production until at least 1938. Two years later it was destroyed by the Luftwaffe in their raid on Coventry.

Although Stevens is the name we normally associate with the production of silk pictures, he had a large number of competitors, notably W.H. Grant, who was to become the mayor of Coventry in 1920. Grant established his business in 1882, when he began weaving silk ribbon bands for the Salvation Army and the Royal Navy, before going on to produce a series of silk portraits in black and white, which he followed by another series, Views of

Old London. Grant and those other relatively unknown silk picture makers such as J.J. Cash and Dalton & Barton, may well become a fruitful field for collectors in the not too far distant future.

If you are going to buy Stevengraphs, it is obviously best to buy those in good condition. Stains and faded silks are going to lower their value considerably, as will missing tassels from bookmarkers. Most Stevengraphs are mounted. If these have obviously been remounted or are badly cracked, these items should also be avoided, unless they are very rare.

As most Stevengraphs are in private collections they are not too easy to come by. They can often by found, however, in the antique markets, particularly at Antiquarius in Chelsea, where Christine Howe at stall M13 generally has a few in stock.

BOOKS

Stevengraphs and Other Victorian Silk Pictures by Geoffrey Godden. This is the definitive work on the subject.
Stevengraphs Price Guide by Austin Sprake.
Stevengraphs by Austin Sprake and Michael Darby.

MUSEUMS

Coventry: Herbert Art Gallery and Museum.
London: Victoria & Albert Museum.

WOVEN IN SILK.

R.M.S. LUCANIA.

SHEFFIELD PLATE

A HAPPY MARRIAGE OF METALS

A late 18th century water jug.

Sheffield Plate was created by the marriage, or fusion, of two metals – copper and silver. The process was discovered about 1704 by an English cutler, Thomas Bolsover.

A traditional story says that when he was repairing a silver knife-handle, he used a copper penny to wedge his vice, and then later discovered that the heat had fused the copper with the silver. Unfortunately for this story, there were no copper pennies around in 1704, so it cannot be true. In fact, no one knows how Bolsover made his discovery, but once made, the result proved to have a great advantage over solid silver if we ignore their respective commercial values. It was not heavily taxed, as was solid silver at the time, and it also meant that such small items as candlesticks, boxes, tableware and a great number of other objects previously made in pure silver, and available only to the rich, became within reach of about a fifth of the price, and still looked very much like the real thing.

An earlier form of silver plating had been attempted earlier by fusing silver with iron or steel, but the process was a failure, as the silver melted when it was heated, and rusted if it became wet.

Not that Sheffield Plate was as perfect a process as it might have been. It was found that years of polishing wore the silver gradually away so that the copper showed through. This problem was solved later by double plating, which began to be used some time after 1765. But single silver plating still continued to be used for the cheaper items, whose interiors were generally tinned to disguise the non-use of silver.

Another problem facing the manufacturers of Sheffield Plate was the tell-tale appearance of copper at the edges where the plate had been cut. This was eventually solved by covering the edges with silver wire.

Embossing produced no problems for the manufacturers as no metal had to be cut away. Piercing a piece of plate was also possible by using a punch after someone discovered that the silver layer was pulled over the copper edge when the punch went through the plate. But engraving *did* present a major problem which could only be partially solved by faintly indenting with a punch so that the silver surface was not broken. Another method was to execute the engraving on a small silver plate and then attach it.

Bolsover, who had started off on a small scale with his discovery by concentrating on the making of buttons and small boxes, sold his business in 1762 to Joseph Hancock, a distant relative and a former apprentice. He had timed his departure from the scene well, as two years later a Birmingham metal manufacturer named Matthew Boulton began producing Sheffield Plate on such a large scale that he was soon its largest manufacturer.

A close friend of Josiah Wedgewood, Boulton was a man of many parts, whose interests included producing ormolu vases for some twelve years before the market collapsed for no apparent reason. He also spent much time and labour on promoting James Watts' steam engine.

While a tremendous variety of domestic objects were coming out of Sheffield and Birmingham, large quantities of plated wares were being imported from France. These were invariably badly plated, and their only dubious merit was that they were even cheaper to buy than those being produced in England. Eventually this was to have a deleterious effect on the quality of Sheffield Plate, as a number of the English manufacturers tried to compete with the inferior French imports by lowering their standards.

It was quite a common practice for manufacturers to stamp their wares with marks that were not dissimilar to silver hallmarks in a deliberate attempt to deceive people, which finally led to a directive being issued which laid down that Sheffield Plate should not be marked in a way that might lead to an item being mistaken for silver — a directive which many manufacturers blithely ignored, even though a fine was imposed.

In 1840 the Sheffield Plate market began to collapse when George and Henry Elkington patented their electro-plating process, an even cheaper method again of producing simulated silver.

It should be added, finally, that it is never advisable to electro-plate a piece of old Sheffield Plate just because it has started to 'bleed', that is to say when the copper has started to show through. This lowers the value of the piece as well as destroying its character.

BOOKS

Antique Sheffield Plate, G.B. Hughes
History of Old Sheffield Plate, R.B. Bradbury
Old Sheffield Plate, E. Wenham

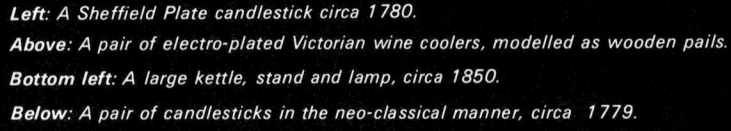

Left: A Sheffield Plate candlestick circa 1780.

Above: A pair of electro-plated Victorian wine coolers, modelled as wooden pails.

Bottom left: A large kettle, stand and lamp, circa 1850.

Below: A pair of candlesticks in the neo-classical manner, circa 1779.

PHILLIPS